# French Food in FRANCE

RICHARD BINNS

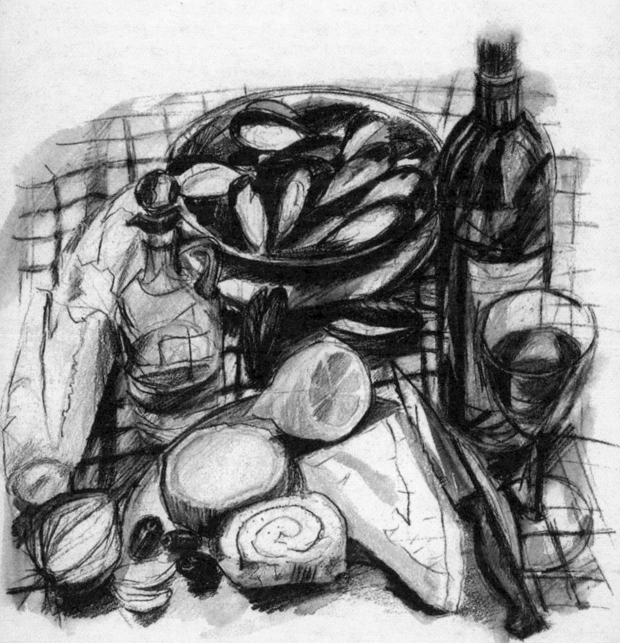

## *How to use* French Food in France

*French Food in France* is the ideal size for everyday use in restaurants, shops and market places. Use the *Glossary of Menu Terms*; refer to the lists of cheeses and specialities detailed in each region; study the wine notes in each regional chapter; and capitalise on both the *Index of Wines* and the *Index of Cheeses* – in France and at home.

Try to study a menu before you enter a dining room (if you are staying overnight ask for a menu long before you go down to the restaurant); this will allow you as much time as possible to do any translation work beforehand. (See page 15 for the phrase you need.) If you are unable to do this do not feel you have to rush to order: take your time and only order when you have translated everything!

Read the introductory chapters before you start your holiday: *Enjoying the best of French cuisine* explains the various types of French cooking; *Wines of France* offers an easy-to-understand analysis of the many hundreds of French wines; *Specimen Letters of Reservation & Useful Phrases* will help you time after time in hotels and restaurants; and, finally, read *A day in the life of a chef and his wife* – it brings to your notice facets of the day-to-day life of hardworking French chefs and their wives which you, the reader, may never have considered before.

I suggest, too, you study *So you think you know that road sign?* (pages 94/95) – it's full of surprises; and make profitable use of *What Wines with What Food* (pages 86/87). Page 47 provides you with helpful advice on making phone calls, the best maps to use, and lists addresses of the more important French Tourist Offices. See also page 31 – *Entente Cordiale – Dead or Alive?*; page 39 – *Books to Take to France*; page 53 – *Tears of Glory*; page 57 – *Times and Holidays*; page 61 – *Pen Pictures – some of the great names of French gastronomy;* and page 85 – *Aperitifs, Wines and Waters* – a guide to the basic types.

## *Maps*

The regional maps identify wine villages and wine-producing areas. Examples • *Madiran* *Jurançon*
Cheese-producing areas are also highlighted. Example: IRATY
Towns and rivers shown for reference purposes are identified as follows: **• Bordeaux • Agen • Pau Adour Gave de Pau**

Typeset by Art Photoset Limited, 64 London End, Beaconsfield, Bucks
Printed in Great Britain by Richard Clay Limited, Bungay, Suffolk.
Distributed in the United Kingdom by the Publishing Division of The Automobile Association, Fanum House, Basingstoke, Hampshire RG21 2EA
Waymark is an imprint of The Automobile Association

Revised edition 1989
First published in 1985 by Chiltern House Publishers Limited as *Bon Voyage*

Published by The Automobile Association
ISBN 0 86145 780 3
AA ref: 10100

# Contents

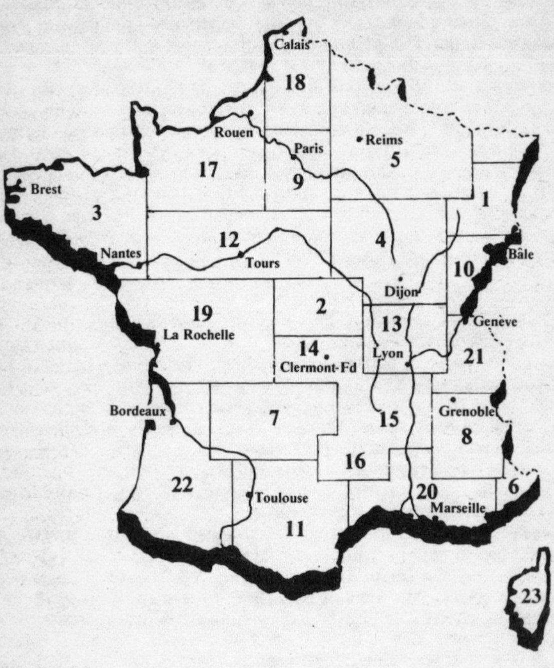
Calais
18
Rouen
Paris
Reims
5
17
9
Brest
3
1
12
4
Nantes
Tours
Bâle
10
Dijon
19
2
La Rochelle
13
Genève
14
Lyon
21
Clermont-Fd
Bordeaux
7
15
Grenoble
8
16
22
20
6
Toulouse
Marseille
11
23

## *Enjoying the best of French cuisine*

Interestingly, 60 years ago, Curnonsky – the French gastronome and writer – identified the four quite different types of French cuisine: *la haute cuisine*; *la cuisine Bourgeoise*; *la cuisine Régionale*; and *la cuisine Improvisée*. He also emphasised that good cooking resulted when 'ingredients taste of what they are.'

Six decades later, and allowing myself some licence, I could say that nothing has changed. Certainly the term *la cuisine Improvisée* was coined long before *la nouvelle cuisine* became so fashionable, though the latter's emphasis on natural-tasting ingredients – and improvisation – represents two of its most important aspects. Curnonsky would relish present trends.

It is my hope that the notes that follow will interest the most experienced Francophiles and those of you who have yet to make your first trip to France. I must stress that they are very much my own personal points of view.

## *Nouvelle Cuisine* – or *Cuisine Moderne*

What is it? In the 1970s Frédy Girardet, in conversation with Craig Claiborne, said this: "*La nouvelle cuisine* is nothing more than good taste. It is to prepare dishes to preserve their natural flavours and with the simplest of sauces."

Today it has moved on to a style that the great French chefs now call *cuisine moderne* – a marriage of the best of classical cuisine and the much abused (by some chefs) and much misunderstood (by many clients and writers) *nouvelle cuisine*. Some call it *cuisine libre* (free cooking); Girardet calls it *la cuisine spontanée* (spontaneous).

It is utterly different from classical cuisine (*la haute cuisine*); for far too long chefs blindly attached themselves to the rules of the old ways, established over many generations and culminating in the work and writings of Escoffier at the turn of the century. Ironically though, it was Escoffier himself who wrote the two priceless words that epitomise what *nouvelle cuisine* is all about – *faites simple*. Escoffier was a creative genius and he established many of the vital principles of good cooking that are still valid today. Most chefs acknowledge this.

Sadly, *nouvelle cuisine* is misunderstood by many visitors to France. For years dire predictions have been made for its early demise. But it is flourishing strongly and, despite some chefs who get it a bad name from time to time, it is likely to become increasingly established.

Why has this happened? I wrote some time ago that Fernand Point was the first to see that times were changing. As far back as 1925 he had realised that his customers had smaller appetites and were concerned about their health and their diets. His menus changed from day to day and depended entirely on what he had bought in the markets; he began the move towards lightness and simplicity, away from the heavy sauces and huge helpings of the past. He trained many of today's great masters: Bocuse, Outhier, Chapel, Vergé and Pierre Troisgros among them.

Simplicity is the key. In its purest, simplest form, *nouvelle cuisine* allows the basic ingredients to count most; the emphasis is on highlighting one natural flavour at a time. Mercifully portions border on the frugal – though this can be torture for those with old-fashioned appetites. Fast cooking is everything – whether it be fish, veal, *foie de canard* or vegetables: steaming, together with poaching and baking, are vital methods of preparation, slow cooking and dishes requiring vast lists of ingredients are not. Flour is all but banned; paper-thin *feuilletés* appear everywhere – no wonder, as they require so little flour.

Sauces, as developed for classical cuisine, are a thing of the past; old chefs would not acknowledge the modern-day, light reductions as sauces at all. These are no more than the concentrated juices of the food released during cooking. Butter, cream and wine are still used – but not to any great excess.

Are mistakes made? Of course they are: far too many superb vegetables are puréed into a sort of baby-food mush – often they all taste the same; helpings can still be too large – particularly the pig trough-like *grand dessert*; vegetables have been duplicated from one course to another at even the most famous restaurants; and combinations of food can sometimes be nauseating. Witness, as examples, the following: Chapel with what was literally a mixed grill of various parts of a lamb – truly awful; Vergé's *loup* and *endive* (the latter was inedible); Mathy's (Belfort) mixture of duck's liver, raspberry vinegar, strawberries, sliced apple and a cut-out bit of toast shaped like a duck!

Apart from in the great restaurants, kitchen staffs are small – often no more than three or four individuals. Machines, therefore, are essential in the kitchens of *nouvelle cuisine* practitioners: food processors; micro-wave ovens; ice cream and sorbet makers, and dry steam ovens. In the hands of skilled chefs the results are never slapdash; they go to considerable pains to get perfection, and presentation of the dishes is done by the *cuisiniers* in the kitchen – it's not left to a careless waiter to destroy their efforts in the dining room. You should never finish a meal feeling bloated – you can fulfil Brillat-Savarin's most famous bit of advice, universally ignored, to leave the table with an appetite. Consequently, what would otherwise appear to be a daunting obstacle, is now a pleasure – a *menu dégustation*; five to eight courses made up of very small helpings of the chef's specialities. It requires great discipline and organisation in the kitchen to prepare and present a well-balanced *menu dégustation* for clients; many of the great chefs fight shy of this – offering all sorts of excuses for not doing it.

Many people confuse *nouvelle cuisine* with *cuisine minceur* (slimming cuisine); one writer even thinks that Guérard won his third star for his *minceur* menus. *Nouvelle cuisine* is hardly calorie free: *cuisine minceur* requires the use of practically no butter, little cream, fat, oil or egg yolks and certainly no flour or sugar; only Guérard can make it reasonably interesting.

Finally, let me explain, in an unusual way, what the greatest benefit of all is – the complete freedom it has given chefs to be creative and brilliantly inventive. If you study really old editions of Michelin, it will soon become crystal clear that the classical cuisine of those days meant repetitive specialities in every town in France. Now look at today's guide. Hundreds of specialities are listed – endless variations based on dozens of basic products; indeed many of the menu decoder books on the market are a waste of money as they cannot help you to translate the menu descriptions. Some of the descriptions are amazing – often extending to 24 words to describe a dish (Chapel and Vergé are the worst culprits). Others cheat by using culinary terms to describe concoctions for which they were never intended; I have seen *saucisson* and *andouillette* used for fish dishes.

The very simplicity of *nouvelle cuisine* is its greatest pitfall; originality is not enough – talent and technique are just as important. Some chefs are incapable of rising to the test; it would be best if they did more to promote real regional cuisine rather than giving *nouvelle cuisine* a bad name or, worse still, sticking to the easy life of cooking *cuisine Bourgeoise* dishes.

## *Regional Cuisine*

In 1980 I wrote that 'there has been a considerable move to preserve and encourage regional specialities.' Now, years later, after spending many, many months of each year in France, driving tens of thousands of miles, and eating at hundreds of restaurants, I have to conclude that the evidence I found on my travels all adds up to a different conclusion; times have changed.

Regional cuisine in provincial restaurants – using old regional specialities – is withering away in most areas of France. Gault Millau are too optimistic about its strength; even Jean Didier (ex-editor of the now defunct Kléber Guide) was woefully short of the mark in suggesting that regional cuisine was making a strong comeback. I know of only one writer who agrees with me – Anne Willan of La Varenne Cookery School in Paris. (Her superb book – *French Regional Cooking* – is the epitome of what a book 'packager' – Marshall Editions Ltd. – can do.) The endless books on French regional cooking (and glossaries) list speciality after speciality but you'll not see them in many provincial restaurants – if at all. I feel that French chefs (particularly those who find *nouvelle cuisine* difficult and who run simpler restaurants) could do far more to research and promote regional specialities, rather than the repetitive, impersonal dishes that predominate in *cuisine Bourgeoise*. Thankfully, there are some chefs who make a superhuman effort to protect regional specialities.

If I had my way, the works of Elizabeth David, Anne Willan and Jane Grigson would be compulsory reading for chefs (with translators at hand). More often than not it's the *charcutier*, *pâtissier* and *boulanger* who keep local traditions alive.

What you will find though in all the French regions is the magnificent use that chefs make of local produce and raw materials – in each of the four different types of cuisine. In the next three pages it is this aspect of regional cooking that I emphasise; referring also to the specialities that you are likely to find in **restaurants** – not those in cookery books, many of which seem to have been taken from ancient reference books. Please also refer to the lists of specialities in each region – again the ones your are likely to be offered in **restaurants**.

Surprisingly, it is becoming more and more difficult for chefs, looking for the best quality and variety of produce, to obtain it locally; frequently they have to buy it from Rungis (the great Paris wholesale market near Orly Airport) – because the best local produce has been swallowed up by the buying methods of centralised distribution systems. An example is in the North – where the best fish, the best of local potatoes and other vegetables are to be discovered at Rungis, not in nearby markets.

In the notes that follow on the cuisine of each region, I examine first the French regions with Atlantic seaboards – starting in the north on the Belgium border and finishing at the Spanish frontier; then the regions that border Belgium, Germany, Switzerland, Italy and the Mediterranean; and, finally, the many differing regions making up the vast mass of inland France. As I consider each region in turn, please refer to the map on page 3; the identifying numbers I use with each regional heading correspond to those shown on that page.

In the following three pages I do not refer to the individual cheeses of each region, though there is a short introduction to cheeses on page 10. I would ask that you read, within the introduction to each region, the details listed on cheeses.

Equally, the same goes for the country's wines, liqueurs and brandies; please read the comprehensive notes detailed in each regional introduction and on pages 85, 86 and 87.

**North** (18) Fish takes pride of place – freshly landed at the ports of Boulogne, Calais and smaller ones like Le Crotoy. *Sole, turbot, maquereaux, barbue, lotte de mer, flétan, harengs, merlan, moules, crevettes* – all appear on menus. So do soups and stews – many with root vegetables: *waterzooï* – fish or chicken stew; *hochepot* – meat and vegetable *pot-au-feu*; *carbonnade* – beef stew with beer. Leeks are superb – enjoy *flamiche aux poireaux* (*quiche*-like pastry). Seek out the *hortillonages* (water-gardens) of Amiens and their young vegetables. Try *gaufres* – yeast waffles and *ficelles* – pancakes with various stuffings. Beer is excellent.
**Normandy** (17) Land of cream, apples and the pig. Vallée d'Auge gives its name to many dishes – including chicken, veal and fish; it means cream, apples or cider, or apple brandy (Calvados) have been added. Cider is superb. Pork products are everywhere: *andouilles* – smoked sausages, eaten cold; *andouillettes* – grilled sausage of pork and veal. Fish are superb: *sole à la Normande, à la Dieppoise, à la Fécampoise, à la Havraise* (the last three are ports); *plats de fruits de mer*; shrimps; oysters; *bulots* (whelks); mussels – and all the treasures from the seas. Enjoy tripe; *ficelles* – pancakes; cow's milk cheeses; butters – salty and sweet; salad produce and potatoes from Caux; exquisite apple tarts; *canard à la Rouennaise*; and fish stews.
**Brittany** (3) Fish and shellfish are commonplace: lobsters, *huîtres, langoustes*, crabs – of varying sorts, *moules*, prawns, shrimps, *coquilles St-Jacques*; to name just a few. Enjoy *cotriade* – a Breton fish stew with potatoes and onions; *galettes* – buckwheat flour pancakes with savoury fillings; *crêpes de froment* – wheat flour pancakes with sweet fillings; *far Breton* – a batter mixture with raisins; *gâteau Breton* – a mouthwatering concoction; *agneau de pre-salé* – from the salt marshes near Mont-St-Michel (fine omelettes are also made there); and *poulet blanc Breton*. It's also one of France's market-gardens: artichokes, cauliflowers, peas, beans, onions and strawberries.
**Charentes/Vendée** (19) – western half of Poitou-Charentes. La Rochelle is a great fishing port; consequently fish predominates – oysters are magnificent (see the brief notes on page 60). The port of La Cotinière, on the island of Oléron, is famous for its shrimps. Challans – in the Vendée – is world renowned for its ducks. Charentes is reputed for its butter, cabbage, goat's milk cheeses, Charentais melons, Cognac, mussels and salt-marsh lamb from the hidden fen country of the Marais Poitevin.
**Southwest** (22) One of the great larders of France – it can be divided into several distinct areas. From the countryside that lies in a semicircle to the north-west, west, south and south-east of Bordeaux comes: lamb from Pauillac; oysters (*gravettes*) from Arcachon; eels; beef (*entrecôte Bordelaise* is the best-known version); onions and shallots; *cèpes*; *alose* (shad); and *lamproie* – lamprey (eel-like fish). The Garonne Valley is one of the orchards of France: prunes from Agen; peaches; pears and dessert grapes. South of the Garonne is **Gascony**: famous for *foie gras* (both ducks and geese); *confit* (preserved meat from both these birds); jams and fruits; and its Armagnac. Try a *floc* (see page 68). To the south and west of Gascony are **Béarn** and the **Landes**. From the latter come *palombes* and *ortolans*, ducks and chickens. Among traditional Béarn specialities are *garbue* – the most famous of vegetable soups; *poule au pot* – the chicken dish given its name by Henri IV; *tourin, ouliat* and *cousinette* (*cousinat*). See the Southwest specialities for further details.
West of Béarn is **Basque** country: tuna, anchovies and sardines are excellent; salmon (from Béarn also), Bayonne ham, *piperade*,

*ttoro* (fish stew) and *gâteau Basque* (pastiza) – try them all.
**Champagne-Ardenne (5) Ile de France (9)** Many of the specialities listed earlier in the North appear in this region, which is renowned for its potatoes and turkeys. In the Ardenne you'll enjoy smoked hams – sold in nets; *sanglier*; *marcassin*; and red and white cabbages. West of Verdun, at Ste-Menehould, try *pieds de cochon* (pig's trotters); *petits gris* (snails); and the many differing sweets and sugared almonds (Verdun is famous for them). Troyes is famous for pork *andouillettes*.
Regional specialities are all but non-existent in the Ile de France – though there are many restaurants in Paris serving the best dishes of all the French regions. Enjoy the *pâtés* and *terrines* and the offerings of the many *pâtissiers* and *charcutiers*.
**Alsace (1)** There is a strong German influence in much of the cooking; pork, game, goose and beer are common. *Foie gras* (fattened goose liver) is magnificent; so, too, are a range of fruits – used in tarts (*linzertorte* – raspberry or bilberry open-tart; *flammekuchen* – flamed open tart), jams, fruit liqueurs and *eaux-de-vie* (see Alsace wines). Stomach-filling *choucroute* and local sausages are on all menus; as are *kougelhopf*, *beckenoffe* and *lewerknepfle* (see regional specialities). Enjoy *tourte Alsacienne* – pork pie; drink beer with it.
**Lorraine** on the north-west borders is known for its *madeleines* (tiny sponge cakes), its *macarons*, its super *quiche Lorraine*, its fruit tarts, its omelettes and its *potée*.
**Jura (10)** This is dairy country – witness the cheeses in the regional introduction. Try *Jésus de Morteau* – a fat sausage smoked over pine and juniper; *brési* – wafer-thin slices of dried beef; and many local hams. *Morilles* and other fungi are common – so are freshly-caught trout and other freshwater fish.
**Savoie (21) Hautes-Alpes (8)** *Plat gratiné* applies to a wide variety of dishes – it always means 'cooked in breadcrumbs'; *gratins* of all sorts show how well milk, cream and cheese can be combined together. Relish *fondue* and *gougère*. Freshwater lake fish are magnificent – see the regional introduction for Savoie. Walnuts, chestnuts, all sorts of fruits and marvellous wild mushrooms are other delights.
**Côte d'Azur (6) Provence (20)** A head-spinning kaleidoscope of colours and textures fills the eyes: aubergines, peppers, tomatoes, cauliflowers, asparagus, beans, olives, garlic, artichokes, courgettes – the list is endless. Fruit, too, is just as appealing: melons from Cavaillon; strawberries from Monteux; cherries from Remoulins; glacé fruit from Apt; truffles from Valréas. Fish from the Mediterranean are an extra bonus: *bar* and *loup de mer*, *daurade*, superb *St-Pierre*, monkfish and mullet – these are the best. Lamb from the foothills of the Alps near Sisteron; herbs of every type from the *département* of Var; honey and olive oil; *ratatouille*; sardines; *saucisson d'Arles*; *bouillabaisse* (see page 32) and *bourride*; *soupe de poissons* and *soupe au pistou*; what memories are stirred as I write!
**Corsica (23)** Relish game and *charcuterie: prissuttu* – raw ham, like Italian *prosciutto; figatelli* – grilled pig's liver sausage; *lonzu* (*lonza*) – slice of pork pickled in salt and herbs; *coppa* (*copa*) – pork sausage or shoulder of pork. Chestnut flour is used in many ways – particularly desserts. Fine citrus fruits and, befitting the island of the *maquis*, superb herbs.
**Languedoc-Roussillon (11) Cévennes (16)** The same products – and dishes – listed in the previous section are available here. Also oysters and mussels from the lagoons (particularly Bouzigues – Thau lagoon; see map page 62). Excellent, too, are a

variety of shellfish. Apricots and pumpkins flourish. *Brandade de morue* (salt cod) appears frequently – as do *confit d'oie* (and *canard*), *cassoulet* and *saucisses de Toulouse*.

**Loire (12)** The river and its many tributaries provide *alose*, *sandre*, *anguille*, carp, perch, pike, salmon and *friture*. A tasty *beurre blanc* is the usual accompaniment for fish. *Charcuterie* is marvellous: *rillettes*, *rillons*, *andouillettes*, *saucissons*, *jarretons* – and other delights. Cultivated mushrooms come from the limestone caves near Saumur.

The **Sologne** is famous for its asparagus, frogs, game, freshwater lake and river fish and wildfowl. You'll be offered, too, many a *pâté*, fruit tarts (it's the home of *tarte Tatin*) and pies.

**Burgundy (4)** Refer to the often seen regional specialities. Many dishes are wine based: *coq au Chambertin* and *poulet au Meursault* are examples. Enjoy hams, freshwater fish, vegetables, *escargots*, mustard and gingerbread from Dijon and blackcurrants (used for *cassis* – the term for both the fruit and the liqueur made from them).

**Lyonnais (13)** The culinary heart and stomach of France – there is a variety of superb produce on hand: Bresse chickens (*chapons* – capons – are unforgettable treats); *grenouilles* and game from Les Dombes; Charolais cattle from the hills north of Chauffailles; freshwater fish from the rivers and pools (pike *quenelles* appear everywhere); *charcuterie* from Lyon – particularly sausages called *rosette* and *saucisson en brioche*; *cervelas* (saveloy); chocolate and *pâtisseries* from Lyon.

**Auvergne (14) Ardèche (15)** Both areas that keep alive old specialities. Refer to the regional lists but here are the best of them: *potée Auvergnate* – a stew of cabbage, vegetables, pork and sausage; *friand Sanflorin* – pork meat and herbs in pastry; *aligot* – a purée of potatoes, cheese, garlic and butter; *pounti* – a small egg-based savoury soufflé with bacon or prunes; and delectable *charcuterie* – hams, *saucisson*, *saucisses sèches* (dried sausages), *pâtés* and so on. The quality and variety of cheeses are magnificent. Cabbages, potatoes, bacon and cheese feature on menus. The area around Le Puy is famous for its lentils and Verveine du Velay – yellow and green liqueurs made from over 30 mountain plants. Fine chestnuts are found in the hills of the Ardèche (relish *marrons glacés*).

**Berry-Bourbonnais (2) Poitou (19)** – eastern half of Poitou-Charentes. The flat terrain of Berry-Bourbonnais is dull country – the granary of France. It's known, too, for its beef, deer, wild boar, rabbits, hares, pheasants and partridge.

Much of Poitou lies in the deserted countryside of Limousin (as do the western edges of the Auvergne). Apart from the specialities listed look out for *mique* – a stew of dumplings; *farcidure* – a dumpling, either poached or sautéed; and *clafoutis* – pancake batter, poured over fruit (usually black cherries) and baked. Limousin is reputed for its *cèpes* – fine, delicate flap mushrooms; and also for its reddish-coloured breed of cattle.

**Dordogne (7)** A land of truffles, geese, ducks, walnuts, *cèpes*, chestnuts and fruit of all types. *Foie gras* of both goose and duck is obligatory on menus; as are *confits* of both birds (preserved in their own fat) and *magrets* (boned duck-breast meat), which have become popular in the last decade throughout France. *Pâtés* incorporating either poultry or game – and truffles – are common. If you see *miques* (yeast dumplings) or *merveilles* (hot, sugar-covered pastry fritters) on menus – order them. In the south – in the Garonne and Lot Valleys – it's a land of orchards: plums, prunes, figs, peaches, pears and cherries.

## *Classical Cuisine*

Henri Gault once claimed that classical cuisine was based on recipes and techniques developed in order to conserve food without the help of refrigeration and to mask food that had already gone bad. *Nouvelle cuisine* requires fresh produce – menus are consequently short and revolve around the chef's purchases each day at the market. Compare that approach with old menus which offered clients scores, if not hundreds, of dishes. How fresh could that produce have been?

Classical French cuisine – *la grande cuisine* – started 450 years ago when Catherine de Medici came to France to become Queen; she brought with her a dozen or so Italian chefs from Florence. Just over 250 years later the developing art came to a standstill with the storming of the Bastille. In 1800 *la grande cuisine* re-emerged and Antonin Carême takes most of the credit for establishing it as the greatest cuisine of its time; in his day ice was not used to keep food fresh – raw materials were either smoked, salted or preserved in vinegar. At the start of the 20th century Escoffier – with the advantage of being able to use refrigeration – took classical cuisine to its supreme peak.

And there it remained; the basic repertoire of hundreds of sauces and garnishes hardly changed – it all became a rigid set of rules, which required faithful copying and little else. Raw materials were obliterated by an excess of butter, cream, alcohol, *foie gras*, truffles, onions, mushrooms, cheese and anything else that could disguise natural tastes.

I hope I do not appear, like Henri Gault, to be too cynical; that would be unfair because over the years my wife and I have enjoyed many of the great classical dishes – and still do. But we do admit, without any hesitation, that simplicity and freshness – in any form of cooking – attracts us far more.

## *Cuisine Bourgeoise*

This is the simple cooking that the majority of French chefs offer to visitors; to their credit it is invariably done well, using good produce, either from the locality or elsewhere in France. More often than not it represents value for money. The repertoire sometimes appears to revolve around the same 20 to 30 dishes – wherever you are in France: *terrine*, *jambon*, *truite*, *escalope*, *côte de veau*, *entrecôte*, *gigot*, *côte d'agneau*, *poulet*, and so on. Rarely do you see a *navarin* or a *blanquette*; these are costly to prepare and must be thrown away – if not ordered. Often the more enjoyable alternative is to picnic; then you have the chance to try the appetising alternatives of the *pâtissier*, *boulanger* and *charcutier*. Take a portable cold box – ideal for keeping picnic things cool.

## *Cheeses*

Within each region I have listed most of its cheeses; the well-known ones can be found throughout the country. They are made from the milk of cows (*vaches*), goats (*chèvres*) or ewes (*brebis*). Try all types and don't be prejudiced about them. In any restaurant follow a good French custom of selecting small portions of several varieties (ask for *une bouchée* – a mouthful – or *une petite tranche* – a small slice). Make waiters identify every cheese. Soft cheeses should be soft and creamy (not runny) and if they smell of ammonia, they are off! Blue cheese that is crumbling and falling apart is unacceptable. The right season for the best cheese will depend on two things: when the cows are put out to pasture and how long it takes to make the cheese. Wherever possible, I indicate the best season.

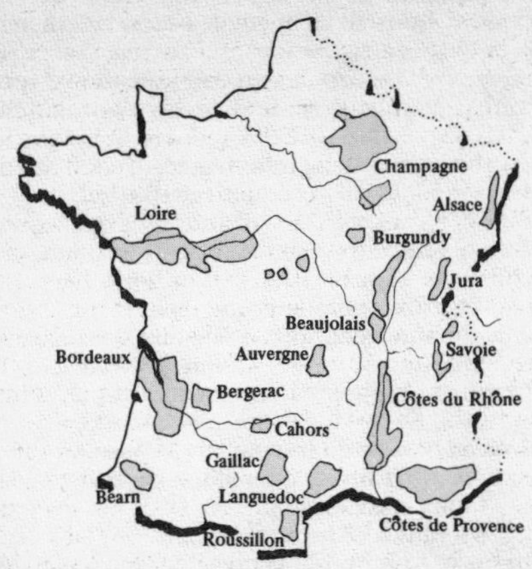


*Main wine-growing areas of France*

Your appreciation and enjoyment of French wines will be greatly enhanced if you understand some basic bits of knowledge.

**Grape types and soil**

One wine will differ from another because it has been made from a different variety of grape. Through hundreds of years of selection and development, each region has its own best single or group of grape varieties. Red Burgundy is made of one grape type, the Pinot Noir. The best white Burgundy is made from the Chardonnay grape (the second rank Burgundy white grape is the Aligoté). Red Bordeaux can come from a variety of grape types: amongst them the Cabernet Sauvignon grape, the Cabernet Franc grape, the Merlot and the Malbec. Cabernets give wine which matures later; Merlot is ideal for quick-developing wine. Blending allows wines to be produced which provide either characteristic: clearly, when long-lasting potential is wanted (particularly for the great Médoc wines), the Cabernet vines predominate; in Saint Emilion the Merlot is widely used.

You should recognise some of the important grape types: the two kinds of Cabernet, Gamay and Pinot Noir (red wine grapes); Riesling, Sauvignon Blanc, Sémillon, Chardonnay, Gewürztraminer (Traminer) and Muscat (six white wine grapes). I refer to these ten, plus several others, throughout the regions.

In some regions you will see a few wines described by their grape type name – *varietal* wines: Gamay (the Beaujolais grape) will appear in the Loire, in Savoie, in the Ardèche and elsewhere; Chardonnay will appear in the Lyonnais, in Champagne country and in obscure wine areas like Poitou. All the wines of Alsace take their names from the grape type used.

Bear in mind that apart from the differing grape vines, the type of soil in which they are grown plays the major part in determining the quality and status of French wines (climate plays another important part). That is why in Burgundy there are so many differing AC classifications – soil can vary from one acre to the next. That is also the reason why the Gamay wines, so delightful in Beaujolais, are never quite matched in other parts of France where the Gamay vine has been planted.

## The main classifications

In every region I list the local wines. Most of them are AC (*Appellation d'Origine Contrôlée*) or VDQS (*Vin Délimité de Qualité Supérieure*) wines; these classifications are shown clearly on bottle labels – the AC is always known as *Appellation Contrôlée* – and they mean that the authenticity of each wine is guaranteed by the French Government and, in addition, the AC or VDQS identifies each wine to its precise birthplace. There are many hundreds of wines with the AC and VDQS guarantee and all but one or two of them are mentioned within the pages of this book. To win these classifications each wine must match its pedigree: specific area, specific grape type or types, maximum yield per acre, minimum alcohol content and so on. Liken the AC wines to the First and Second Division Football League clubs (they can vary from the very best of the First Division to the worst teams of the Second Division): the VDQS wines are the Third Division ones – and, believe me, a few of these Third Division wines, on their home grounds, are perfectly capable of beating some of their big brothers!

## Identifying the wines of France

I have tried to make it as simple as possible for you to identify all the wines of France. You may be in a restaurant in France (**or anywhere else in the world**) with a wine list in your hand, or, you may be back home, wanting perhaps to locate a specific wine before buying it. **Use the index at the back of the guide** – this lists hundreds of wine names (see page 308). It includes all the AC and VDQS wines of France, together with most of the more common *Vins de Pays* (explained later). It also includes most of the important village names which, themselves, take the AC or VDQS classification of the region (this is particularly true in the south). Throughout France you can often be confused by this method of description – reference to many of the starred restaurants in the Michelin guide will illustrate what I mean: do you know **Bruley**, **Bué**, **Mareuil** or **Taradeau** wines?

In the regional texts on wines all these hundreds of varieties have been shown in **bold** print, so, whenever you see a label name on a wine list, it will be easy for you to quickly identify it and to find its birthplace on the regional map.

## How does the Appellation Contrôlée system work?

Let us consider Beaujolais wines as a way of explaining the AC system; the same logic applies in the other wine-making areas of France. Beaujolais is the area north of Lyon and south of Mâcon on the west side of the River Saône (see map on page 174). From the hills in that area come lovely, fresh, light red wines, all made from the Gamay grape. If you see a bottle with an **Appellation Beaujolais Contrôlée** label, the wine could have originated in any part of the Beaujolais area. It will be a *generic* wine, both cheaper and of a lesser quality than the following wines.

If the label states **AC Beaujolais Villages**, the wine will have been made in any one of the thirty or more villages in the north of the Beaujolais region which have not yet earned their own AC status. It will be a superior wine to the previous one.

If the words say **AC Brouilly**, the wine will have come from the *commune* of Brouilly itself (one of the eight Beaujolais villages that have their own AC classification); if the wine has originated from the hillsides of Mont Brouilly, the label would say **AC Côte de Brouilly**, the ninth individual AC of the area. Often the best vineyards are on the *côtes* (sides). Finally, if the label has the addition of **Château Thivin** to the words **AC Côte de Brouilly**, this will be wine from the best estate on the Mont.

Generally speaking, the larger the geographic area described on the label, the cheaper and less superior the wine will be.

**VDQS wines**

There are plenty of other good wines in France without the AC classification which are just as appealing and enjoyable – and less expensive. The main category below AC is VDQS, made by producers who are working hard to earn their own AC status. Examples are **Minervois** and **Corbières**, red wines originating from Languedoc-Roussillon.

**Vins de Pays and Vins de Table**

Below the VDQS classification are *Vins de Pays* (liken them to the Fourth Division of football clubs) scattered throughout the country. These meet strict French Government controls; the labels specify precisely from which *département* or, in some cases, from which tiny area they come and the wines must be made from the grape varieties designated by Government order. They must meet minimum alcohol levels (not less than 10 per cent in the South, 9 or 9.5 per cent elsewhere). There are some one hundred possible *Vins de Pays* classifications throughout France – over half of them in the *départements* of Aude, Hérault, Gard and Pyrénées-Orientales (Languedoc-Roussillon). You may never see some of them. I have tried to identify and locate the most common ones; I have a lot of tasting to do . . . why not help me? *Vins de Table* is the lowest category of all – your non-league wines or your supermarket plonk. Some of them, bottled by the best producers – like Listel – are really good; but most are tasteless rubbish. Many of these wines, grown in the vast vineyards of the Midi, are blended with imported Italian wine (France buys vast quantities of it).

**What to order**

Whatever the restaurant, always order local or regional wines: if you explore each region in the way this guide suggests, it will follow, without fail, that you will gain some basic idea of where the main wine-producing areas are situated, the villages within them, and the varying types of wine coming from the local vineyards. It is not imperative to order a wallet-busting bottle of the best Burgundy or Bordeaux *Grand* or *Premier Cru* vintages when you eat at the great restaurants. Alsace, Savoie, Lyonnais, Provence, the Southwest and the Côte d'Azur have their own marvellous local wines and the best of these are on the wine lists of all the great restaurants in each of those regions. It is significant that, during the last decade, many restaurants have been doing far more to promote the unknown, local wines; with the high prices being asked world-wide for Burgundy and Bordeaux vintages this had to happen. This guide will equip you to profit from your knowledge. Don't take wines too seriously – enjoy them, as my wife and I have enjoyed many scores of the local wines recommended in this book.

At the best restaurants take the advice of the *sommelier*. Look for their small lapel badge (a bunch of grapes); they have worked and studied hard to acquire their knowledge of wines. With the aid of this book there is no need to feel intimidated by them.

Essential terms you should understand are: **Brut** very dry; **Sec** dry (*Champagne* – medium sweet); **Demi-sec** medium sweet; **Doux** or **Moelleux** sweet; **Mousseux** sparkling; **Crémant** a little less sparkle; **Pétillant** a slight sparkle; **Perlant (perlé)** a few bubbles; **Cru** growth, as in *first growth* – meaning vineyard status; **Blanc de Blancs** any white wine made from white grapes, rather than white and black. For other useful and interesting information see pages 85, 86 and 87. *Santé!*

**To reserve bedrooms – options on right (in brackets)**

| | | |
|---|---|---|
| 1 | Would you please reserve a room | (2 rooms, etc.,) |
| 2 | with a double bed | (with 2 single beds) (one room with) (each room) |
| 3 | and bathroom/WC | (and shower/WC) (and shower) |
| 4 | for one night | (2 nights, etc.,) |
| 5 | *(indicate day, date, month)* | |
| 6 | | (We would like *pension* (half-*pension*) terms for our stay) |
| 7 | Please confirm the reservation as soon as possible and please indicate the cost of the rooms | (your *pension* terms for each person) |
| 8 | An International Reply Coupon is enclosed | |
| 9 | Yours faithfully | |
| 1 | **Pouvez-vous, s'il vous plaît, me réserver une chambre** | **(2 chambres, etc.,)** |
| 2 | **avec un lit à 2 places** | **(avec 2 lits à une place) (une chambre avec) (chaque chambre)** |
| 3 | **avec salle de bains/WC** | **(et douche/WC) (et douche)** |
| 4 | **pour une nuit** | **(2 nuits, etc.,)** |
| 5 | **le** *(indicate day, date, month)* | |
| 6 | | **(Nous voudrions pension complète (demi-pension) pour notre séjour)** |
| 7 | **Veuillez confirmer la réservation dès que possible, et indiquer le tarif des chambres** | **(le tarif de pension par personne)** |
| 8 | **Ci-joint un coupon-réponse international** | |
| 9 | **Je vous prie, Monsieur, d'accepter l'expression de mes salutations distinguées** | |

**To reserve tables – options (in brackets)**

Would you please reserve a table for __ persons for lunch (dinner) on *(indicate day, date, month)*. We will arrive at the restaurant at *(use 24 hour clock)* hours. (We would like a table on the terrace.) Please confirm the reservation. An International Reply Coupon is enclosed. Yours faithfully

**Pouvez-vous me réserver une table pour __ personnes pour déjeuner (dîner) le. Nous arriverons au restaurant à heures. (Nous aimerions une table sur la terrasse.) Veuillez confirmer la réservation. Ci-joint un coupon-réponse international. Je vous prie, Monsieur, d'accepter l'expression de mes salutations distinguées**

**Useful Phrases – General**

Can I have **Puis-je avoir**; Can we have **Pouvons-nous avoir**; an (extra) pillow **(encore) un oreiller**; a blanket **une couverture**; a towel **une serviette**; some soap **du savon**; heating **le chauffage**; a laundry service **une blanchisserie**; some hot (cold) milk **du lait chaud (froid)**;

a knife **un couteau**; a fork **une fourchette**; a spoon **une cuiller**; a bottle of . . . **une bouteille de** . . . a half-bottle of . . . **une demi-bouteille de** . . . the wine list . . . **la carte des vins** . . .

an ashtray **un cendrier**; a glass **un verre**; a plate **une assiette**;

Fill the tank up (petrol). **Faites le plein**

Check the oil, please. **Vérifiez l'huile, s'il vous plaît**

May I park here? **Puis-je me garer ici?**

Get a doctor. **Appelez un médecin**

**Useful Phrases – at the hotel**
Can I have **Puis-je avoir**; Can we have **Pouvons-nous avoir**; I would like **Je voudrais**; We would like **Nous voudrions**; May I have some . . . **Pourrais-je avoir . . .**;
May I see the room? **Puis-je voir la chambre?**
No, I don't like it. **Non, elle ne me plaît pas**
What's the price . . . ? **Quel est le prix . . . ?**
Do you have anything . . . ? **Avez-vous quelque chose . . . ?**
better **de mieux**; bigger **de plus grand**;
quieter **de plus tranquille**; cheaper **de moins cher**;
Haven't you anything cheaper please? **N'avez-vous rien de moins cher, s'il vous plait?**
Fine – I'll take it. **D'accord – je la prends**
What is the price for full board (half-board)? **Quel est le prix pour la pension complète (demi-pension)?**
I would like a quiet room, please. **Je voudrais une chambre tranquille, s'il vous plaît**
Can we have breakfast in our room? **Pouvons-nous prendre le petit déjeuner dans la chambre?**
Please telephone this hotel/restaurant and reserve a room/a table for me. **Pouvez-vous, s'il vous plaît, téléphoner à cet hôtel/ce restaurant et me réserver une chambre/une table**
Would you recommend the best local *pâtissier/charcutier/boulanger*? **Pouvez-vous me recommander le meilleur pâtissier/charcutier/boulanger du coin?**

**Useful Phrases – in the restaurant**
Can I have **Puis-je avoir**; Can we have **Pouvons-nous avoir**; I would like **Je voudrais**; We would like **Nous voudrions**;
Could we please have . . . **Pouvons-nous avoir . . . s'il vous plaît**
We would like to have a look at the fixed-price menu, please. **Nous voudrions voir le menu à prix-fixe, s'il vous plaît**
What's this? **Qu'est-ce que c'est que ça?**
Would you please recommend your regional specialities? **Pourriez-vous nous recommander les spécialités de la région, s.v.p?**
We would like to share this speciality between us, please. **Nous aimerions partager cette spécialité entre nous, s'il vous plaît**
May we change this speciality for another one? **Est-ce que nous pouvons changer cette spécialité pour une autre?**
Which local wines would you recommend that we try? **Quels vins du pays nous recommanderiez-vous d'essayer?**
Please do not serve us big portions. **Ne nous servez pas de trop grosses portions, s'il vous plaît**
That is not what I ordered. I asked for . . . **Ce n'est pas ce que j'ai commandé. J'ai demandé . . .**
rare **saignant**; medium-done **à point**; well-done **bien cuit**;
Could you bring another plate, please? **Pourriez-vous apporter une autre assiette, s'il vous plaît?**
Would you please identify your local cheeses? **Pouvez-vous nous donner les noms de vos fromages du coin, s.v.p?**
May we have decaffeinated coffee, please? **Pouvons-nous avoir du café décaféiné, s'il vous plaît?**
May we please see your kitchens after our meal? **Serait-il possible de visiter les cuisines après le repas, s.v.p?**
May we please see your wine cellar after our meal? **Serait-il possible de visiter la cave après le repas, s'il vous plaît?**
Would you give us the address of your wine merchant? **Pourriez-vous nous donner l'adresse de votre marchand de vins?**
Would you give us the name of your cheese supplier? **Pourriez-vous nous donner le nom de votre fournisseur en fromages?**

## *A day in the life of a chef and his wife*

Jean was half-awakened by the shrill rattle of the alarm clock – it was 5 a.m. He raised one eyelid, then closed it; momentarily he slipped again into the enveloping arms of half-conscious sleep – the sudden realisation that it was Tuesday brought him sharply to his wide-awake senses.

How he hated Tuesday – the start of his six-day week after the blessed relief of a lazy Monday. He slid gently out of bed – Jacqueline was oblivious to the noisy alarm. Quietly he tiptoed past the rooms of his young children. A cold shower took two minutes of his time, he dressed quickly and skipped shaving – he had to arrive at the market by 6.00, 70 kilometres away.

The Renault 18 Estate moved silently and swiftly along the deserted, misty roads – it was May and just getting light. Jean had plenty of time to reflect on his lot in life. At 34 he had already made a name for himself; Gault Millau, with an enthusiastic recommendation, had given him a flying start three years earlier, a year after he and Jacqueline had bought the old auberge. Two months ago the first Michelin star had shone above the auberge – it had been a proud day for them. At last those 12 years of working at Roanne, Crissier and London had paid off.

The market was busy and crowded. Juggernauts had already arrived from all parts of France: they had brought fish and shellfish from both the Atlantic and Mediterranean ports; fresh spring vegetables and fruit from Provence; cheeses, butter and cream from Normandy; and poultry, *grenouilles*, *cailles* and *pigeons* from Bresse. Jean moved rapidly around the market – apparently relaxed, but missing nothing, and with the time to exchange greetings with his important suppliers; they, too, were proud to share in his success. His final purchases were armfuls of flowers; Jacqueline prided herself on her displays.

By 7 a.m. he had left the market and already he had a working outline of what that day's menus would be. On the drive back to the auberge he clarified his thoughts; he changed his three fixed-price menus and his à la carte menu every day. A master stroke had been the purchase of a small word processor a year earlier: within its memory it already had stored the menu descriptions of many scores of his specialities; he could manually add any new creation of his in a few seconds. Each day, after giving his 'toy' some simple instructions, it would whistle out as many copies of his menus as he required – rapidly, neatly and with a professional print-like presentation. It made the art of being a skilled *nouvelle cuisine* chef so much easier – though he prided himself that his menus always included a few regional favourites.

At 8.00 he arrived back at the auberge; Jacqueline and the youngsters were up and about and for twenty minutes they shared an animated breakfast. Then she whisked them away to school, to return as quickly as she could to ensure that their 16 bedrooms were all spic and span before the first guests of the week arrived, later that day; Tuesday was the only day each week when there were no guests requiring breakfast.

A second, more leisurely shower left Jean refreshed and ready for the battle of the week ahead. His first job was to ensure that his three kitchen staff were hard at work. He gave them a quick idea of what the menus would be and he saw to it that they made a start on as much of the preparatory work as possible. Jean was a particularly skilled *pâtissier* and took great care in the preparation of his appetisers, superb desserts and delectable *petits fours*. To complicate matters Jean baked his own bread – offering six varieties to his clients at both lunch and dinner.

By mid morning he was free to play with his word processor

'toy'. Occasionally it would break down – then all hell would let loose. This Tuesday it went well. For the first time that day he remembered that a *cuisinière* colleague – on her day off – was paying him a visit for lunch. She was 10 years older than Jean and was now known throughout France as one of the few top lady chefs. He admired her greatly; she had brought up two children – they were now in their teens – and she had a husband who supported her efforts with fantastic enthusiasm. Jean shook his head in awe at the energy she managed to find each day; the same was true – to a lesser extent – of Jacqueline.

He decided on the spur of the moment that he would use his visitor as a guinea pig for a new speciality he had perfected. Each year Jean spent his annual holiday in February visiting the legendary chefs; in Burgundy he had relished a new cheese course offered by Marc Meneau and called a *feuilleté de fromage chaud sur salade*. Jean had experimented for months to create his own version; he would prepare that especially today and see what reception it would receive from his visitor and her husband.

At 11.30 Jean and Jacqueline joined the kitchen staff and their four young waiters for their own hurried lunch. It gave him the chance to encourage and – without them knowing it – influence his staff, in myriad ways; the couple placed great emphasis on all of them being friendly, knowledgeable and watchful. By midday they were ready for their clients.

Jacqueline supervised the ordering of the *apéritifs*, dishes and wines. Most of the specialities were prepared at the last minute, the most severe test of discipline being the critical timing needed to prepare and present the seven courses making up the *menu dégustation*. The restaurant could seat 50 people; often, more than half of Jean's clients would order the *dégustation* menu – all sitting down at different starting times.

Relentlessly the minute kitchen got noisier, more chaotic and hotter; occasionally tempers flared briefly. Periodically each of the kitchen staff needed to retire outside for a few seconds to gasp in some cool air. As the pressure eased Jean visited the dining room to have just a brief chat with his clients: today he gave a warm welcome to his special guest.

At 4.00 Jean was welcoming his bank manager – he needed to ask for a further loan of 200,000 francs. He had not had the good fortune to inherit a family hotel free of debt; everything the couple possessed had to be paid for and already they had long-term debts of over a million francs. Now they needed to extend the kitchen and continue the task of renovating their bedrooms (their plans included the task of adding a bathroom to each one). With the French economy floundering and with sky-high interest rates, Jean felt he was walking on a bed of razor blades at times; interest charges were one of his biggest overheads.

An hour later he had his loan. Then his wine merchant arrived. Jean's magnificent wine cellar – with more than 10,000 bottles – was a huge drain on his capital, but he considered it an absolutely vital investment. He spent another 50,000 francs on wine.

That evening the whole hectic cycle was repeated – with the added complication of welcoming overnight guests. At 7.00 Jean snatched a few brief minutes with his children before they went up to their rooms; then followed another few hours of energy-sapping effort. After their guests retired, Jacqueline, too, went up to bed. 11.30 saw Jean with his staff deciding what tomorrow's purchases would be.

A few minutes before midnight Jean slipped quietly into bed – as silently as he had risen from it, 19 hours earlier.

# ALSACE

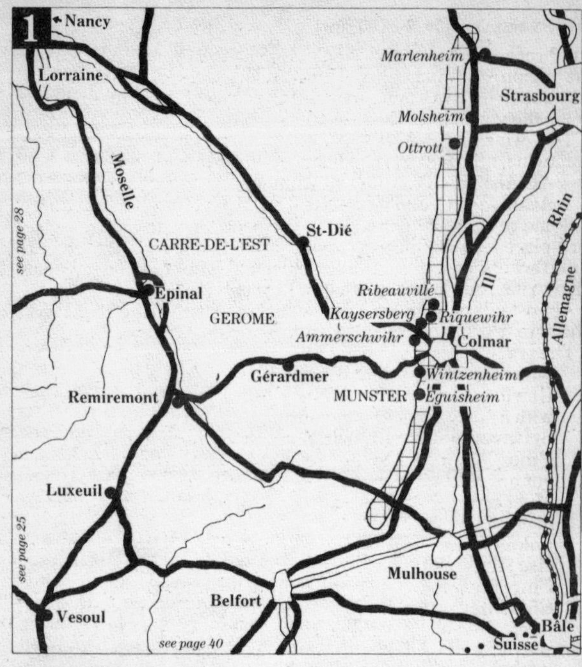


## *Cheeses* Cow's milk

**Carré-de-l'Est** soft, edible, white rind, made in a small square; milder than Camembert. Bland taste. Available all year

**Gérardmer** same cheese as Gérômé, alternative name

**Géromé** soft, gold-coloured cheese, a little more solid than Munster, often covered with fennel or caraway. Made as a thick disk. Spicy taste and at its best in summer and autumn. Good with full-bodied red wines

**Munster** soft, gold-coloured, stronger taste than Gérômé, made as a small disk. Munster *Laitier* (made by commercial dairies) available all year. *Fermier* (made by farms) at its best in summer and autumn. Try them with **Traminer** wines. **Munster au cumin** (with caraway seeds)

## *Regional Specialities*

**Beckenoffe** a stew, or hotpot, of potatoes, lamb, beef, pork and onions, cooked in a local wine

**Choucroute garnie** sauerkraut with peppercorns, boiled ham, pork, Strasbourg sausages and boiled potatoes. Try it with a beer (*bière*)

**Chou farci** stuffed cabbage

**Foie gras** goose liver

**Kougelhopf** a round *brioche* with raisins and almonds

**Krapfen** fritters stuffed with jam

**Lewerknepfle (Leber Knödel**) liver dumpling (pork liver dumpling)

**Matelote Alsacienne** in Alsace made with stewed eels (in the past from the River Ill) – sometimes with freshwater fish

**Pflutters Alsacienne** potato puffs

**Potage Lorraine** potato, leek and onion soup

**Schifela** shoulder of pork with turnips

**Tarte (aux mirabelles)** golden plum tart. Also with other fruits

**Tarte à l'oignon Alsacienne** onion and cream tart

*Wines* *best years* **79 81 83 85 86 87**

Until recently there was a single Appellation Contrôlée (AC) for the region, **AC Alsace** (or **Vin d'Alsace**). A few years ago an additional AC was announced, **AC Alsace Grand Cru**; these being the wines from the best vineyards.

The wines of Alsace take their names from the type of grapevine; followed by the village or winegrower's name.

**AC Alsace – Traminer d'Ammerschwihr** (village name)

**AC Alsace Grand Cru – Riesling Hugel** (producer's name)

Some restaurants will identify the best wines to their precise birthplace by indicating vineyard names – examples: **Kaefferkopf** (south of Ammerschwihr); **Schoenenbourg** (near Riquewihr); **Schlossberg** (east of Kaysersberg).

Almost all the wines are white but some are pink or light red. They are dry, fresh and fruity – a few are ideal dessert wines.

The grape types are:

**Riesling** for dry white wine

**Gewürztraminer** (**Traminer**, for short) dry white wine, with a spicy scent and flavour

**Sylvaner** a light, tart, workhorse grape for white wine

**Pinot Blanc** or **Klevner** related to the Chardonnay grape, but not as good; a fresh, aromatic white wine

**Muscat** dry, white wine and with a perfume fit for your handkerchief!

**Tokay dAlsace** for spicy, full-bodied white wine – known also as the **Pinot Gris** grape type. Needs ageing

**Pinot Noir** for rosés and light red, full-bodied wines

**Chasselas** an inferior white grape with no flavour. Now rarely seen in Alsace, being replaced by the Pinot Blanc

Wines with the **AC Vin d'Alsace-Edelzwicker** label are the most basic of Alsace wines, made from a mixture of grape types, usually Sylvaner and Pinot Blanc; they are fruity and light whites. Rarely seen is a white **Crémant d'Alsace** (it represents about one per cent of Alsace production). Alsace wines are sold in distinctive green bottles, called *flûtes*.

Don't miss any of the Alsace brandies – called *eaux-de-vie*. These are colourless liqueurs distilled from fermented fruit juices: *kirsch* – cherry; *framboise* – raspberry; *prunelle* – sloe; *mirabelle* – golden plum; *quetsche* – purple plum; and *myrtille* – bilberry (blueberry). Look out for brightly-coloured fruit liqueurs; these are macerated – hence their lovely colours.

# BERRY-BOURBONNAIS

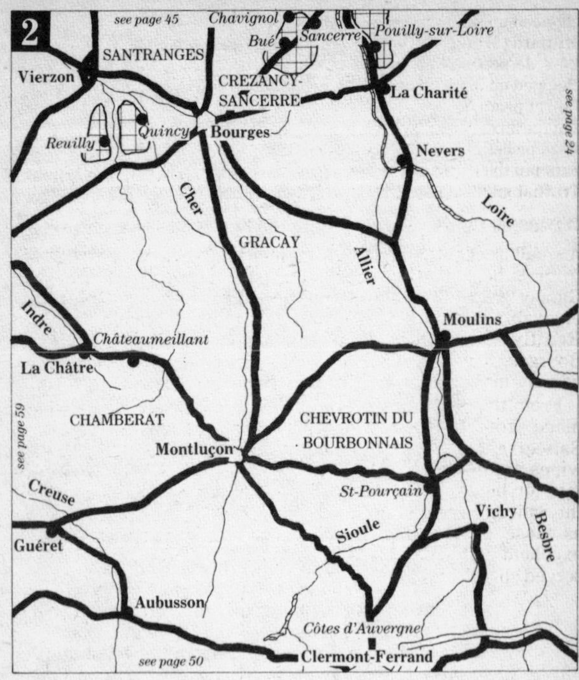


## *Cheeses* Cow's milk

**Chambérat** is a fruity-tasting cheese – made as a flat, pressed disk. Ideal with **St-Pourçain** wines

### Goat's milk

**Chevrotin du Bourbonnais** a truncated cone and creamy tasting. Best in summer and autumn. Also known as **Conne**

**Crézancy-Sancerre** small ball – similar taste to Chavignol (see Loire cheeses). **Santranges** is a related, similar cheese

**Crottin de Chavignol** from the area just west of **Sancerre**, which, with **Chavignol**, makes the ideal wine to accompany it. It takes the form of a small, flattened ball. In grilled form it now appears regularly throughout France as a hot cheese course. The best season is winter

**Graçay** is a nutty, soft cheese – made as a dark blue-coloured cone

Also see the cheeses listed in the Loire – page 44.

## *Regional Specialities*

**Bignons** small fritters

**Bouquettes aux pommes de terre** grated potato, mixed with flour, egg white and fried in small, thick pieces

**Brayaude (gigot)** lamb cooked in white wine, onions and herbs

**Chargouère (Chergouère)** pastry turnover of plums or prunes

**Cousinat (Cousina)** chestnut soup (*salée* – salted) with cream, butter and prunes – served with bread

**Gargouillau** a *clafoutis* of pears

**Gouéron** a cake of goat cheese and eggs

**Gouerre (Gouère)** a cake of potato purèe, flour, eggs and *fromage blanc*, cooked in an oven as a *tourtière*

**Lièvre à la Duchambais** hare cooked slowly in a sauce of cream,

chopped-up shallots, vinegar and pepper
**Milliard** (**Millat – Milla**) a *clafoutis* of cherries
**Pâté de pommes de terre** a tart of sliced potatoes, butter, bacon and chopped-up onions, baked in an oven. Cream is added to the hot centre
**Poirat** pear tart
**Pompe aux grattons** a cake, in the shape of a crown, made of a mixture of small pieces of pork, flour, eggs and butter
**Sanciau** thick sweet or savoury pancake – made from buckwheat flour
**Truffiat** grated potato, mixed with flour, eggs and butter and baked

## *Wines*

A small area but interestingly enough some fine wines originate from its borders. **Châteaumeillant** VDQS reds, made from the Gamay grape, are good; **Vins de St-Pourçain-sur-Sioule** are enjoyable Gamay reds and particularly fine Loire-type whites; **Reuilly** and **Quincy**, small wine-making areas to the west of Bourges, have excellent local reputations for their dry white wines – made from the Sauvignon Blanc grape.

From the banks of the Loire come some lovely, white wines, made from the Sauvignon Blanc grape: **Pouilly-Fumé** and **Sancerre**, both flinty and smoky flavoured. **Pouilly-sur-Loire** wines are made from the same general area, but the wines are inferior, being made from a different grape type, Chasselas. From the Sancerre area come good rosés: often described on wine lists as **Rosé de Bué** and **Rosé de Chavignol**. There's also an excellent red wine, made from the Pinot Noir grape – often served slightly chilled.

# BRITTANY

## *Cheeses* Cow's milk

**Campénéac** a pressed, uncooked cheese. Strong smell and made in thick disks. Good all the year

**Meilleraye de Bretagne** at its best in summer. Light smell, ochre-yellow rind, made in large squares

**Nantais dit Curé (Fromage du Curé)** (**Nantais**) strong smell, supple, small square of cheese. Good all the year

**Port-Salut** is a semi-hard, mild cheese, good all the year. Port-Salut was the monastery where the cheese was originally made – at **Entrammes** (Mayenne); the name was sold to a dairy company, though a variety of the type is still produced there. St-Paulin is a related cheese

**St-Gildas-des-Bois** a triple-cream cheese with a mushroom smell – cylinder shape and available throughout the year

**St-Paulin** semi-hard, yellow, mild, smooth-textured with a washed, bright orange rind. Made commercially throughout northern France: in Brittany, the Loire Valley, Normandy and Champagne-Ardenne

Try any of these cheeses with the reds from the **Coteaux d'Ancenis** or the whites of **Muscadet** or **Gros Plant du Pays Nantais**.

## *Regional Specialities*

**Agneau de pré-salé** leg of lamb, from animals pastured in the salt marshes and meadows of Brittany

**Bardatte** cabbage stuffed with hare – cooked in white wine – and served with chestnuts and roast quail

**Beurre blanc** sauce for fish dishes; made from the reduction of shallots, wine vinegar and the finest butter (sometimes with dry white wine)

**Cotriade** fish soup with potatoes, onions, garlic and butter

**Crêpes Bretonnes** the thinnest of pancakes with a variety of sweet fillings – often called **Crêpes de froment** (wheat flour)

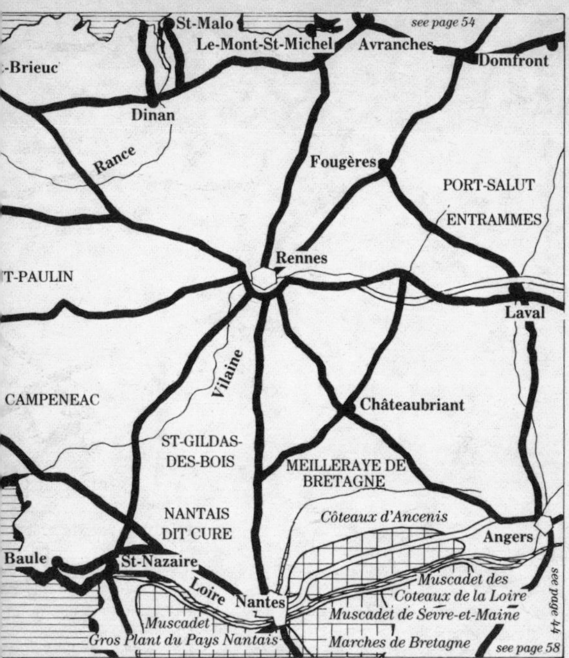


**Far Breton** batter mixture with a raisin filling
**Galette** takes various forms: can be a biscuit, a cake or a pancake; the latter is usually stuffed with fillings like mushrooms, ham, cheese or seafood and is called a **Galette de blé noir** (buckwheat flour)
**Gâteau Breton** thick *galette* (sweet type), flavoured with rum
**Gigot de pré-salé** same as *agneau de pré-salé*
**Paloudes farcies** clams in the shell, with a *gratiné* filling
**Poulet blanc Breton** white Breton chicken. Spend the last few weeks of their lives running free in the meadows

## *Wines*

**Whites** *best years* 85 86 87
Let me be charitable and allow this region to claim **Muscadet** wines, grown on the southern bank of the Loire, near Nantes. The white, very dry and inexpensive white wines are made from the Muscadet grape (hence their name) and are ideal to drink with fish. The AC wines are **Muscadet, Muscadet de Sèvre-et-Maine** and **Muscadet des Coteaux de la Loire**. A junior VDQS cousin is **Gros Plant du Pays Nantais**, made from the Folle Blanche grape. Enjoy, too, the marvellous Breton cider.
**Reds**
A good VDQS red comes from Ancenis (**Coteaux d'Ancenis**), made from the Gamay grape; the area is east of Nantes, on the northern bank of the Loire.
**Vins de Pays**
These are similar to the Muscadet whites and Ancenis reds: they will be classified by *département* – **Maine-et-Loire** and **Loire-Atlantique** or **Vin de Pays des Marches de Bretagne**. Vast amounts are made – lots of it is tasteless rubbish; much of the latter makes its way, sadly, to the U.K.

# BURGUNDY

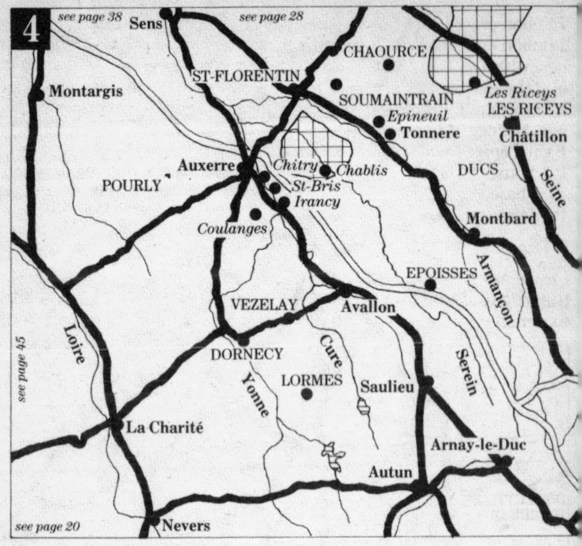


## *Cheeses* Cow's milk

**Aisy-Cendré** cured in **Marc** and stored in wood ashes. Firm, strong-smelling, fruity taste; good with full-bodied red wines

**Boulette de La Pierre-Qui-Vire** amusingly named – made at the abbey of the same name near St-Léger-Vauban. Small, firm ball – herb flavoured

**Chaource** to the west of Les Riceys. At its best in summer and autumn – a creamy cheese, made in cylinders; mushroom smell

**Cîteaux** thick disk, very rare and made by the monks at Cîteaux Monastery – once a rival of Cluny. Cîteaux is to the east of Nuits-St-Georges

**Ducs** from the area of Tonnere; a soft cylinder ideal with **St-Bris** whites

**Epoisses** soft, orange-dusted, made as a flat cylinder. At its best in the summer, autumn and winter and it goes well with full-bodied red wines

**Langres** small, cone-shaped and strong. Related to Epoisses – and is made north of Dijon. Try it with red Burgundies

**Les Riceys** from the borders of Champagne and Burgundy; a still **Rosé des Riceys** comes from the same area and is classified as a Champagne wine. Try it with this soft, fruity-tasting, small disk of cheese

**Rouy** related to Epoisses. Strong smell, soft and made as a square

**St-Florentin** related to Epoisses – as is **Soumaintrain**. Smooth, red-brown small disk with spicy taste. Season summer to winter

### Goat's milk

**Dornecy** just west of Vézelay. Small, firm, upright cylinder

**Lormes** south of Avallon, related to both Dornecy and Vézelay

**Montrachet** soft, mild and creamy – made as a tall cylinder

**Pourly** slight nutty flavour, soft and made as a small cylinder

**Vézelay** a farm produced cheese, at its best in summer and autumn. Soft and in the form of a cone, with a bluish rind

## *Regional Specialities*

**Bœuf Bourguignon** braised beef simmered in wine-based sauce

**Charolais (pièce de)** steak from the excellent Charolais cattle

**Garbure** heavy soup, with mixture of pork, cabbage, beans and sausages

**Gougère** cheese pastry, based on Gruyère cheese

**Jambon persillé** parsley-flavoured ham, served cold in its jelly
**Jambon en saupiquet, Jambon à la crème, Jambon à la Morvandelle** ham with a piquant cream sauce, wine and wine vinegar
**Matelote** freshwater fish soup, usually based on a red wine sauce
**Meurette** red wine-based sauce with small onions. Accompanies fish or poached egg dishes
**Pain d'épice** spiced honeycake from Dijon
**Pochouse (pouchouse)** stew of freshwater fish and garlic, usually white wine based
**Potée** see *Garbure*

## *Wines*

I have asked you to always try local wines; the only difficulty in this region is that some of the locals are the most famous and expensive in the world. Some *Grand Cru* wines, dating back to

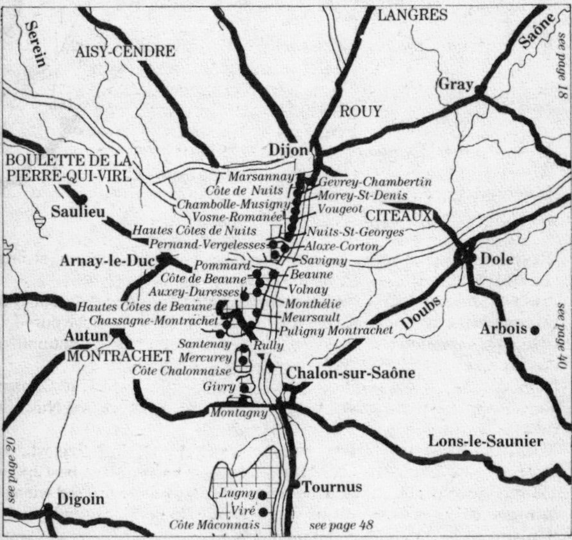


the best vintage years, could cost as much as you are paying for your whole holiday. The simple reason for this is that the Côte d'Or, where the best Burgundy wines come from, produces less than one-tenth of the AC wines of Bordeaux; yet, there is a complex patchwork of many dozens of Appellation Contrôlée classifications, every one of them listed here. All the famous Burgundies, those at the very top of the pyramid, both in quality and price, will have labels that identify them down to the *commune*, followed by the vineyard, *Domaine* or *Clos* itself, some no bigger than a pocket handkerchief. Most of them will have their own AC, whereas in Bordeaux, the famous châteaux share the AC for the local *commune* or region. In Burgundy, the term *Premier Cru* means the second rank vineyards – below the *Grand Cru* top level.

The best red Burgundy is usually less dry and is sweeter than a claret, warm and more full-bodied. The great white Burgundies, rich and dry, are far and away the best whites to drink with food, but most of them are priced out of reach of us all. The groups of AC classifications that follow have all been listed in **north** to

**south** order; this will help you to locate and identify each village, and the estates within them, more readily.

**Famous Reds** *best years* **76 78 79 80 81 82 83 85 86**

This first group are the great red wine *communes*, each with their own AC; in brackets are shown the individual Appellation Contrôlée estates within each village. These are the great wine-producing estates, the *Grand Cru* vineyards:

| | |
|---|---|
| **Gevrey-Chambertin** | **(Mazis-Chambertin, Ruchottes-Chambertin, Chapelle-Chambertin, Griotte-Chambertin, Chambertin Clos de Bèze, Chambertin, Charmes-Chambertin, Latricières-Chambertin, Mazoyères-Chambertin)** |
| **Morey-Saint Denis** | **(Clos de la Roche, Clos Saint Denis, Clos de Tart)** |
| **Chambolle-Musigny** | **(Bonnes Mares, Musigny)** |
| **Vougeot** | **(Clos de Vougeot)** |
| **Vosne-Romanée** | **(Echézeaux, Grands Echézeaux, Richebourg, Romanée-Saint Vivant, Romanée, Romanée-Conti, La Tâche:** these are some of the world's best vineyards) |
| **Nuits-Saint-Georges** | |
| **Aloxe-Corton** | **(Corton, Charlemagne)** |
| **Pernand-Vergelesses** | |
| **Savigny-lès-Beaune** | |
| **Beaune** | |
| **Pommard** | |
| **Volnay** | **(Volnay-Santenots;** not a *Grand Cru* and lying in Meursault) |
| **Monthélie** | |
| **Auxey-Duresses** | |
| **Santenay** | |

**Famous Whites** *best years* **78 79 82 83 85 86**

The following are the famous white wine villages with AC classifications (estates with their own AC are shown in brackets):

| | |
|---|---|
| **Chablis** | To the east of Auxerre; **Grand** and **Premier Cru** classifications |
| **Aloxe-Corton** | **(Corton-Charlemagne)** |
| **Meursault** | |
| **Puligny-Montrachet** | **(Chevalier-Montrachet, Bienvenues Bâtard-Montrachet, Montrachet, Bâtard-Montrachet, Criots-Bâtard-Montrachet)** |
| **Chassagne-Montrachet** | |
| **Pouilly-Fuissé** | Well to the south, near Mâcon |

**Rosés**

Perhaps the best rosé in France comes from **Marsannay**, the village at the northern end of the Route des Grands Crus. It takes the **AC Bourgogne** with the addition of the words **Rosé Marsannay**. A host of general rosé wines have their own AC classifications – all starting with the word **Bourgogne**: **Grand Ordinaire Rosé**; **Ordinaire Rosé**; **Rosé**; **Rosé Hautes Côtes de Beaune**; and **Rosé Hautes Côtes de Nuits.**

**Less-Famous Wines**

The ordinary traveller will have to be content with the wines carrying humbler labels, and thankfully, amongst the dozens of appellations, there are many really good, inexpensive wines like the following examples:

**Reds**

**Bourgogne Ordinaire. Bourgogne Grand Ordinaire** (made from the Gamay grape – the lowest Burgundy Appellation: *Clairet* – this term, if applied to any Burgundy wines, means they will be light red wines). **Bourgogne Passetoutgrains** (a mixture of Gamay – two-thirds – and Pinot Noir – one-third: slightly further up the quality scale). **Bourgogne** – made from Pinot Noir – is an even more highly thought of Appellation and is produced in much the greatest quantities amongst the reds of the area. **Bourgogne Marsannay** and **Bourgogne-Marsannay-la-Côte. Fixin. Bourgogne Hautes Côtes de Nuits. Côte de Nuits (Vins Fins). Côte de Nuits-Villages. Bourgogne Hautes Côtes de Beaune. Ladoix. Chorey-lès-Beaune. Côte de Beaune. Côte de Beaune-Villages. Blagny. Dezize-lès-Maranges. Sampigny-lès-Maranges. Cheilly-lès-Maranges. Mercurey. Givry. Mâcon (rouge). Mâcon Supérieur.**

**Whites**

**Petit Chablis. Bourgogne. Bourgogne Aligoté** (the second rank grape type, but the most common general white Burgundy). **Auxey-Duresses. Saint Romain. Saint Aubin. Rully-Montagny** (the wines of **Buxy** take the AC for Montagny). **Mâcon (blanc). Mâcon-Villages. Pinot Chardonnay-Mâcon** (an example of a *varietal* wine). **Pouilly-Loché. Pouilly-Vinzelles** (these last two villages, just east of Fuissé, are cheaper alternatives to Pouilly-Fuissé; they do not have the right to that famous name). **Saint Véran** (see page 48: several villages straddling Pouilly-Fuissé and including Saint Vérand – note the different spelling – have the right to this AC; again, a similar wine to its famous namesake). Many restaurants in the area describe Mâconnais wines by village names: noteworthy are **Viré** and **Lugny**.

Many of the villages in the lists produce both red and white wines. Remember also that many of the well-known *communes* in the first two lists will have vineyards in them that have the right to claim the AC for the village, but, nevertheless, do not have the reputation of some of their famous neighbours; many of those villages will have excellent wines at much lower price levels.

**Other wines**

If you are based at Avallon, or anywhere in the north of the region, look out for the red **Irancy**, the light **Rosé Irancy** and the crisp, dry, white wine called **Sauvignon de St-Bris**, made in two tiny villages on the eastern bank of the Yonne. Other local villages are **Chitry** and **Coulanges** – their names are often seen on wine lists. Look out, too, for a **Crémant de Bourgogne** or a **Bourgogne mousseux.** Try the **Marc de Bourgogne**, pure spirit, distilled from grapes after the final pressing. Dijon is where Cassis is produced; that rich syrup made from blackcurrants, and, when added to white wine (particularly good with Aligoté) it becomes **Kir**, named after Canon Kir, a mayor of Dijon and a hero of the *Résistance*. With Crémant de Bourgogne – called **Royal Kir**. Relish, too Liqueur de Poires William. (**Clos de la Chainette** is a vineyard in the shadow of Auxerre Cathedral.)

# CHAMPAGNE-ARDENNE

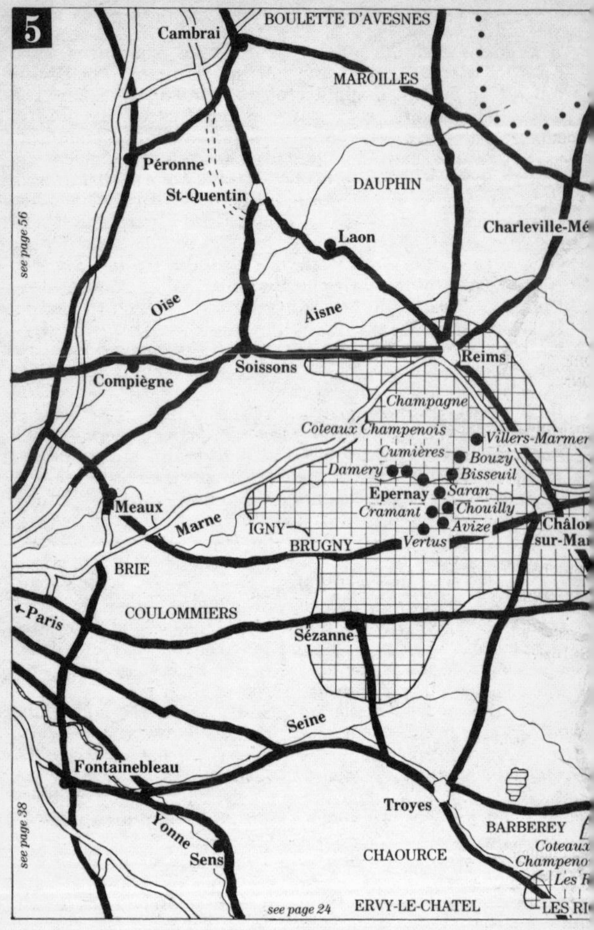


## *Cheeses* Cow's milk

**Barberey** from the area between Chaource and Les Riceys. A soft, musty-smelling, small cylinder. Best in summer and autumn

**Boulette d'Avesnes** soft, pear-shaped and pungent bouquet. Sharp and strong – try it with **Genièvre** (see the North region)

**Brie** soft, white rind, the size of a long-playing record. Try with **Bouzy**

**Caprice des Dieux** soft and mild, packed in oval-shaped boxes

**Cendré d'Argonne** from north of Châlons-s-Marne; soft, ash coated

**Cendré de Champagne (Cendré des Riceys)** mainly from Châlons-s-Marne – Vitry area. Flat disk and coated with ashes

**Chaource** at its best in summer and autumn; a creamy cheese, made in cylinders and with a mushroom smell. From the borders of Burgundy

**Chaumont** related to Epoisses and Langres cheeses (see Burgundy). Cone-shaped, soft cheese with strong smell

**Coulommiers** like Brie, but a smaller, 45 rpm disc. At its best in summer, autumn and winter

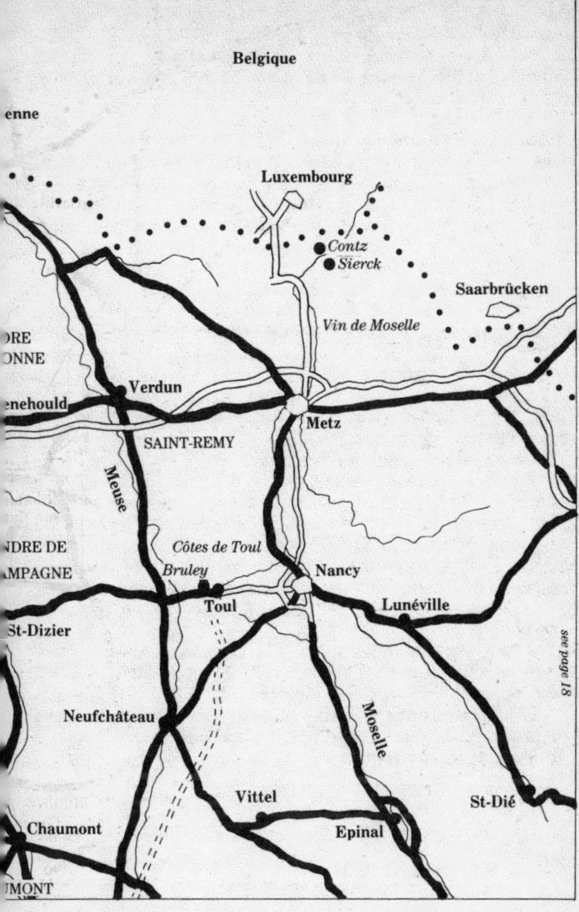


**Dauphin** from the Avesnes area. Soft, seasoned, crescent-shaped, heart or loaf. Is related to Boulette d'Avesnes
**Ervy-le-Châtel** truncated cone – firm with a mushroom smell
**Igny** made by monks at the Igny Monastery – a pressed flat disk
**Maroilles** soft, slightly salty and gold. Appears in many regional dishes
**Les Riceys** from the area south of Troyes, home also of a good **Rosé des Riceys** wine. Best seasons, summer and autumn. Flat disk, no strong smell and fruity taste. Try the local wine with it
**Saint Rémy** a spicy-tasting, strong-smelling, reddish-coloured square

## *Regional Specialities*

**Flamiche aux Maroilles** see *Tarte aux Maroilles*
**Flamiche aux poireaux** puff-pastry tart with cream and leeks
**Goyère** see *Tarte aux Maroilles*
**Hochepot** a *pot-au-feu* of the North (see *Pepperpot*)
**Pepperpot** stew of mutton, pork, beer and vegetables

**Rabotte (Rabote)** whole apple wrapped in pastry and baked
**Sanguette** black pudding, made with rabbit's blood
**Tarte aux Maroilles** a tart based on the local cheese
**Waterzooï** a cross between soup and stew, usually of fish or chicken

*Wines best years* **76 79 81 82 83**

**Champagne** is the only area in France where the AC classification does not have to be shown on the labels of bottles.

A **Crémant de Cramant** (*crémant* means about half the normal bubbles) is a delicious alternative to Champagne. There are many non-sparkling wines from the Champagne area worth looking out for; the broadest classification is **Coteaux Champenois**. Whites from **Cramant**, **Villers-Marmery**, **Avize** and **Chouilly** and a **Rosé des Riceys** (with its own AC – see map) are good. You may also see a **Chardonnay** (the Champagne area white grape), usually carrying a merchant's name (**Saran** – made by Moët & Chandon is one). Other good wines are the reds: a delicate **Bisseuil**; a light **Bouzy**; and those from **Vertus**, **Damery** and **Cumières** (all made from the other important Champagne grape – Pinot Noir). The term **ratafia** describes a mixture of brandy and unfermented Champagne.

The non-vintage, blended Champagnes are always good value; but if you can afford a vintage wine (designated as such by the experts of Champagne) you will readily understand Joseph Krug's famous words: "For vintage Champagne I have to share the credit with God." Be certain to visit the Moët cellars in Epernay – an unforgettable experience, full of interest; and the Pommery or Ruinart cellars (both in the south-east suburbs of Reims) where you can see the amazing underground 'pyramids' – Les Crayères.

To the north-east of the region – in Lorraine country – are two VDQS areas: **Côtes de Toul** (the village name **Bruley** is often used on local lists) and **Vin de Moselle** (from the Metz area – wines made in **Contz** and **Sierck**, both spas, appear on menus); wines of all shades are made in both areas but the dry **Vin Gris** (a pale pink) is the most common.

## *Entente Cordiale – Dead or Alive?*

Since I started writing and publishing books on France I have received several thousands of letters and press reviews from every corner of the globe. One alarming aspect has emerged from some of that correspondence and press comment: all of you seem to love France and accept the proposal that 'Everyone has two countries – his own and France'; but some of you dislike the French a great deal – finding them unacceptably hostile.

The letters and reviews make sad reading: 'on the whole the English like France but not the French' . . . 'haughty superiority' . . . 'the French don't deserve France' . . . 'supercilious' . . . 'unfriendly and bloody-minded' . . . 'thoroughly bad-tempered – as only the French know how to be.'

The French can be enigmatic and contrary, that's for certain; they were voted by North American travel writers to be a nation of people as unfriendly as Russians and Iranians. I myself have had a few thoroughly bad experiences – and, more than once, witnessed some unpleasant treatment being meted out on unsuspecting, innocent visitors. However, I've come across a far, far greater number of exceptional examples of kindness, helpfulness and friendliness and in no way whatsoever can I condone the cruel hostility one seems to encounter these days in the press; I suspect it has become the fashion to knock the French as often and as hard as possible. Much of the criticism is sheer hypocrisy. Are Anglo-Saxons that perfect? Hardly.

The French are a proud, strongly nationalistic race; we should try to copy that patriotism – not deplore it. We should try, too, to emulate their exceptional industry and the great respect they have for the 'family'; and we could also study their turbulent history – no wonder they are suspicious of others.

It would be tragic if France drifted further apart from Britain and her oldest Allies across the Atlantic in North America. Certainly the French themselves could try to tone down what often can be arrogant and unfriendly behaviour; be a little less serious at times and to develop a stronger sense of humour; find out a good deal more about their neighbours; and be less selfish and ruthless in pursuing their own interests.

But I believe even more strongly that **visitors to France should meet the French more than half-way**; they should make an effort to understand some of the language and they should try to seek out and meet more French people – rather than just following the crowded tourist tracks to the same endless ancient monuments. Always begin any conversation – whatever the situation – with a smiling *Bonjour*; the French put a high value on that common courtesy. Visitors should also see more of provincial France where the real heart of the country still beats strongly; and to avoid the cities whose inhabitants are no more nasty than those found in any other metropolitan jungle. Theodore Zeldin, in his book *The French*, wrote: "French people often feel that they are misunderstood by foreigners, that they are insufficiently appreciated, unloved.' They are right; but we must share the blame equally with them for that.

Maurice Buckmaster, the head of the French section of the Special Operations Executive (SOE) during 1941-45, has urged that we all breathe new life into the Edwardian *Entente Cordiale* – signed in 1904. It is incumbent on all of us to do just that – whether we live across the Channel or on the other side of the Atlantic. We must all work harder to improve the harmony between our countries; a family relationship that currently appears to be in a bad state of health and a great deal less cordial than it ought to be. (See page 53.)

# COTE D'AZUR

## *Cheeses* Goat's milk

**Banon** a soft cheese made in a small disk, usually wrapped in chestnut leaves; sometimes *au poivre*, covered with black pepper (see map – p. 63)
**Poivre-d'Ane** flavoured with rosemary or the herb savory (*sariette*). In this form same season as Banon. Aromatic taste and perfume

### Ewe's milk

**Brousse de la Vésubie** from the Vésubie Valley; a very creamy, mild-flavoured cheese

## *Regional Specialities*

**Aïgo Bouido** garlic and sage soup – with bread (or eggs & cheese)
**Aïgo saou** fish soup, without *rascasse*, served with *rouille*
**Aïoli (ailloli)** a mayonnaise sauce with garlic and olive oil
**Anchoïade** anchovy crusts
**Berlingueto** chopped spinach and hard-boiled eggs
**Bouillabaisse** a dish of Mediterranean fish (including *rascasse*, *St-Pierre*, *baudroie*, *congre*, *chapon de mer*, *langoustes*, *langoustines*, *tourteaux*, *favouilles*, *merlan*, and, believe it or not, many others!) and a soup, served separately, with *rouille*, *safran* and *aïoli*
**Bourride** a creamy fish soup (usually made with big white fish), thickened with *aïoli* and flavoured with crawfish
**Brandade (de morue) à l'huile d'olive** a mousse of salt cod with cream, olive oil and garlic
**Capoum** a large pink *rascasse* (scorpion fish)
**Pain Bagna** bread roll with olive oil, anchovy fillets, olives, onions, etc.

**Pieds et paquets** small parcels of mutton tripe, cooked with sheep trotters and white wine
**Pissaladière** Provençal bread dough with onions, anchovies, olives, etc.
**Pistou (soupe au)** vegetable soup bound with *pommade*
**Pollo pépitoria** Provençal chicken *fricassée* thickened with lemon-flavoured mayonnaise
**Pommade** a thick paste of garlic, basil, cheese and olive oil
**Ratatouille** aubergines, courgettes, onion, garlic, red peppers and tomatoes in olive oil
**Rouille** orange-coloured sauce with hot peppers, garlic and saffron
**Salade Niçoise** tomatoes, beans, potatoes, black olives, anchovy, lettuce and olive oil. Sometimes tuna fish
**Tapénade** a purée of stoned black olives, anchovy fillets, capers, tuna fish and olive oil
**Tarte (Tourte) aux blettes** open-crust pastry with filling of Swiss chard (not unlike Chinese cabbage) and pine nuts
**Tian** Provençal earthenware dish

## *Wines*

To the west of this region, and in the Var Valley, lie several wine-producing areas. The wines are fresh and fragrant – they have two per cent more alcohol than their northern cousins.

They are usually white or rosé; a few reds are produced, notably the excellent **Château Vignelaure** (see page 63) – a smooth, full-bodied wine. **Cassis, Bandol, Bellet** (near Nice), **Coteaux d'Aix-en-Provence, Côtes de Provence** are amongst the AC and VDQS classifications. Many of the latter wines carry village names on their bottle labels: **Pierrefeu, Cuers** and **La Londe** (all near Hyères); **Le Beausset** and **La Bégude** (near Aix-en-Provence); **Vidauban, Taradeau, Les Arcs** and **Trans** (south of Draguignan); **Gassin** – you may also see **Château Minuty**, a Gassin property, near St-Tropez. In Nice you may see **Château de Cremat** (the best Bellet wine); menus will list producers' names – like Listel or L'Estandon. See map page 63.

# DORDOGNE

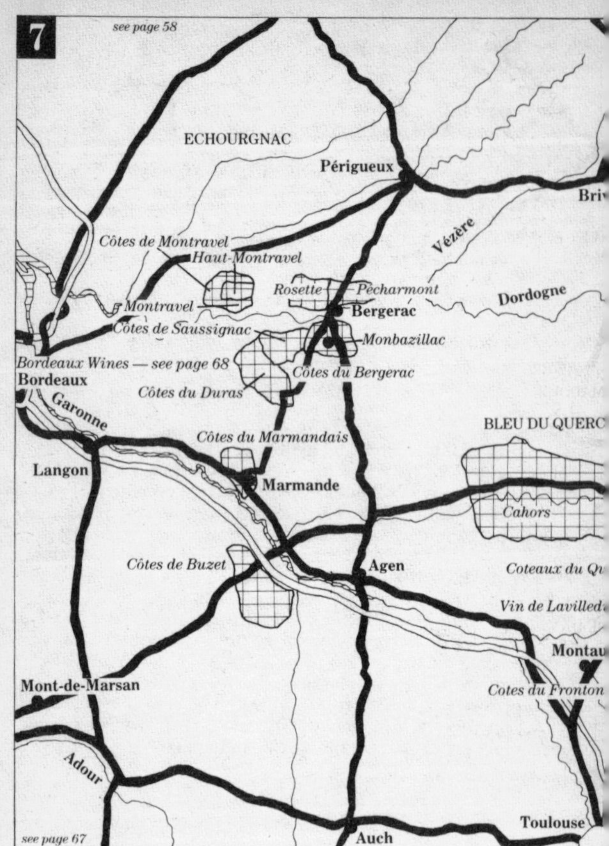


## *Cheeses* Cow's milk

Many of the cheeses listed come from the Massif Central:

**Auvergne (Bleu d')** when made on farms at its best in summer and autumn. Strong smell, soft, made in the same way as Roquefort

**Cantal** from the Auvergne. Semi-hard, nutty flavour. Praised by Pliny; the best comes from Salers (**Fourme de Salers**). Also known as **Cantalon** and **Fourme de Rochefort**. *Fourme* is an old word describing how the cheeses were formed

**Causses (Bleu des)** a blue cheese with parsley-like veins, hence the term *persillé* – often used to describe a blue cheese. At its best in summer and autumn. **Bleu du Quercy** is a related cheese

**Echourgnac** pressed, uncooked, small disk – made by monks

**Fourme-d'Ambert** a summer and autumn season. A blue cheese from the Auvergne and in the shape of a tall cylinder

**Laguiole** related to Cantal. Big cylinders, penetrating bouquet

**Murol** a semi-hard cheese, like St-Nectaire. Made in small disks, mild with no special smell

**Passe-l'An** made as a huge wheel – a strong, hard cheese

**St-Nectaire** a purply-brown skin, made in larger disks than Murol. Semi-hard, mild cheese

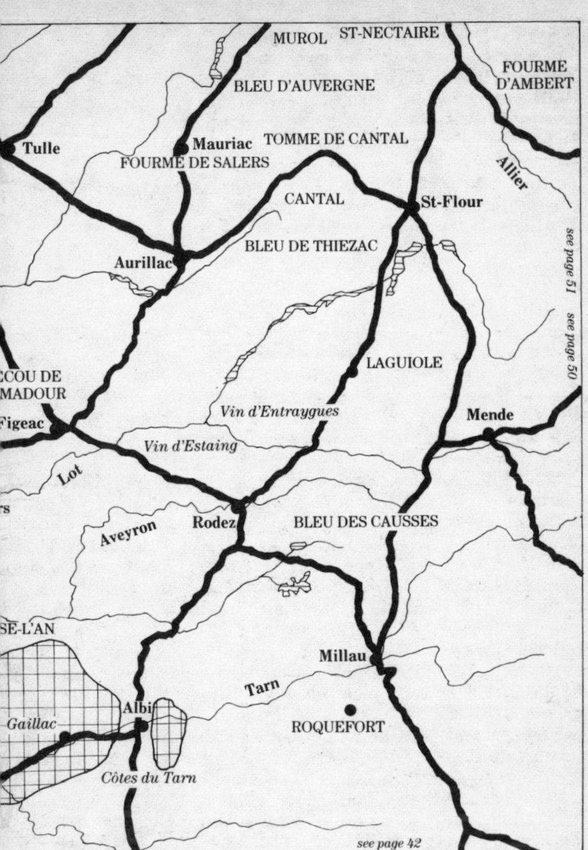


**Thiézac (Bleu de)** at its best in summer and autumn. A blue cheese related to Bleu d'Auvergne

**Tomme de Cantal** a fresh, softish, cream-coloured, unfermented cheese; used in many Auvergne regional dishes

### Goat's milk

**Cabécou de Rocamadour** gets its name from the patois for *little goat*. Very small size with nutty taste. At its best in summer and autumn

### Ewe's milk

**Roquefort** the best blue cheese of all. Sharp and salty. See notes in Massif Central. Try it with a local red wine **Cahors** – or surprise yourself with an accompanying sweet **Sauternes**

## *Regional Specialities*

**Bourrioles d'Aurillac** sweet pancakes, made from buckwheat flour
**Cèpes** fine, delicate mushrooms. Sometimes dried
**Chou farci** stuffed cabbage. Sometimes *aux marrons* – with chestnuts
**Confit de canard (d'oie)** preserved duck (goose)
**Cou d'oie** neck of goose
**Foie de canard (gras)** duck liver (goose)
**Friands de Bergerac** small potato cakes

**Merveilles** hot, sugar-covered pastry fritters
**Mique** stew or soup with dumplings
**Pommes à la Sarladaise** potatoes, truffles, ham or *foie gras*
**Rillettes d'oie** soft, potted goose
**Sobronade** soup with pork, ham, beans and vegetables
**Tourin Bordelais (Ouillat)** onion soup
**Tourin Périgourdine** vegetable soup
**Truffes** truffles; black and exotic tubers or fungi, as large as walnuts, they grow on the roots of certain oak and hazelnut trees
**Truffes sous les cendres** truffles, wrapped in paper (or bacon) and cooked in ashes

## *Wines*

### Reds

There are many good local wines made in the region itself. From **Bergerac** and the **Côtes de Bergerac** (circling the town, both north and south of the River Dordogne) come some fine wines; light-weight, claret-type reds. Similar wines are made in the **Pécharmant** area and the **Côtes de Duras** (south of Bergerac). **Sigoulès** and **Leparon** are Côtes de Bergerac wines.

### Whites

Amongst the whites, look out for **Bergerac sec, Côtes de Bergerac, Côtes de Duras** and **Rosette** – all ideal for fish and entrées. Across the Dordogne from Bergerac is the *commune* of **Monbazillac**, where the famous, sweet, heady dessert wine is made; another sweet wine is **Côtes de Bergerac moëlleux**. From the **Côtes de Montravel, Montravel, Haut-Montravel** (three different areas) and the **Côtes de Saussignac** come medium-sweet whites; and a few dry whites.

### Other Wines

Further south from the Dordogne itself are the wines of **Cahors** – full-bodied dark reds plus the white, **Blanc du Lot**. **Gaillac** makes reds, whites, rosés, plus the sparkling whites, **Gaillac mousseux** and **Gaillac perlé**; **Gaillac Premières Côtes** and **Gaillac doux** are medium-sweet whites. The town is on the Tarn (between Toulouse and Albi) and its wines have a pedigree going back to 920 A.D. Some good red and white VDQS wines are made in the Lot Valley, south of Montsalvy: **Vin d'Estaing** and **Vin d'Entraygues et du Fel**. North of Toulouse are the AC **Côtes du Frontonnais** (its main centre is **Villaudric**); good reds are made here. West of Cahors is the **Côtes du Marmandais** area and its reasonably good light reds and whites. Another light VDQS red comes from south of Cahors, called **Vin de Lavilledieu**.

All the wines of **Bordeaux**, detailed in my description of the Southwest (page 69), can be enjoyed here in the Dordogne. Many of the best are made on the banks of the River Dordogne, just before it flows into the Gironde.

### Vins de Pays

Good examples flourish in this region. **Coteaux du Quercy** and **Côtes du Tarn** offer wines of all shades; *département* labels will say **Lot, Lot-et-Garonne** and **Tarn-et-Garonne.**

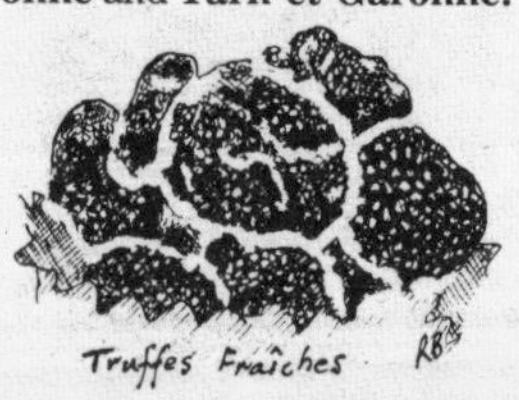

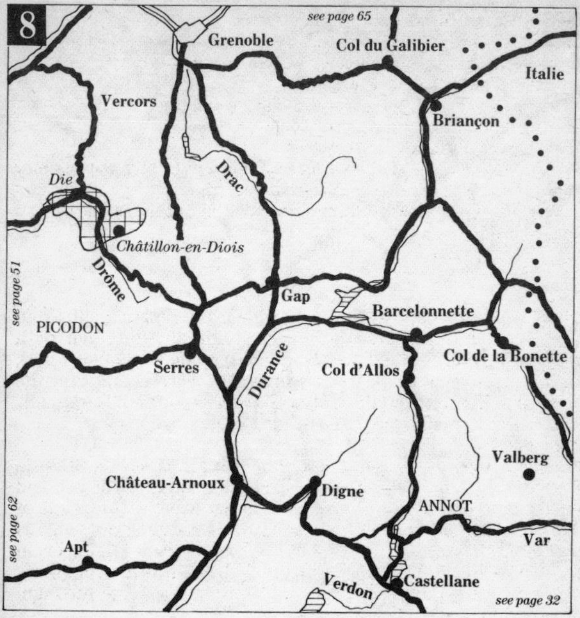

8

see page 65
Grenoble
Col du Galibier
Italie
Vercors
Briançon
Drac
Die
Châtillon-en-Diois
Drôme
see page 51
Gap
PICODON
Barcelonnette
Serres
Durance
Col d'Allos
Col de la Bonette
Valberg
Château-Arnoux
Digne
ANNOT
see page 62
Var
Apt
Verdon
Castellane
see page 32

## *Cheeses*

See also the cheeses listed in the Savoie region.

**Annot (Tomme d'Annot)** a nutty-flavoured, pressed disk; made from ewe's or goat's milk

**Picodon** is a goat cheese; soft, mellow taste and doughnut size. Various sources – Diois (see map) and Rhône Valley

## *Regional Specialities*

See those listed in the Savoie region.

## *Wines*

Enjoy the light wines from Savoie (see page 66), from Provence (see pages 33 and 64) and from the **Côtes du Rhone** (see pages 62 and 63).

In Die you will find the lovely *demi-sec* **Clairette de Die** (made by a local, *naturel* method from mainly Muscat grapes) and a *brut* version (made by *méthode champenoise* from Clairette grapes); both wines are **mousseux**. There's a dry still white, too. Near Die are the wines of all shades from **Châtillon-en-Diois**.

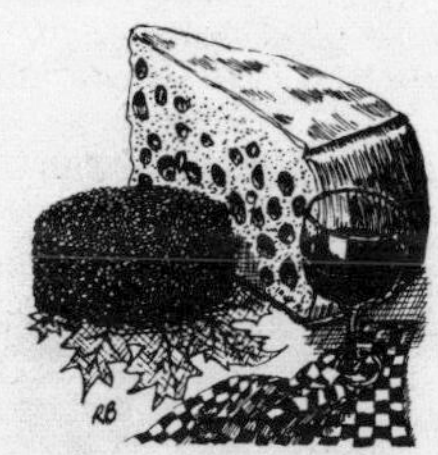

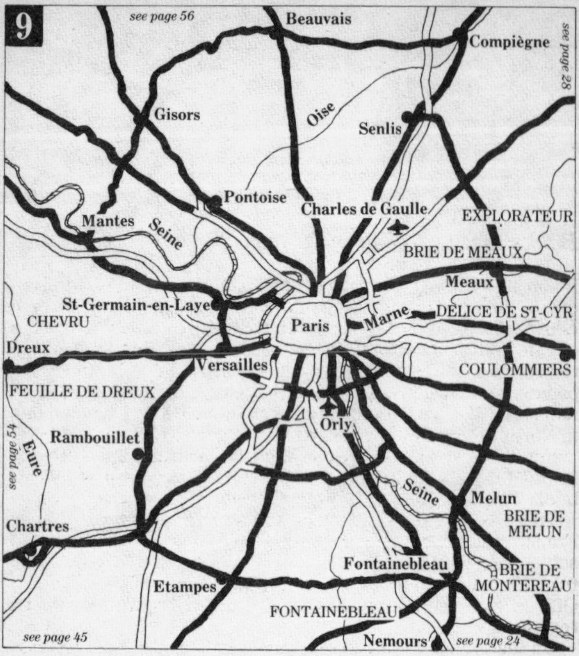

# ILE DE FRANCE

9

see page 56
Beauvais
Compiègne
see page 28
Gisors
Oise
Senlis
Pontoise
Charles de Gaulle
EXPLORATEUR
Mantes
Seine
BRIE DE MEAUX
Meaux
St-Germain-en-Laye
CHEVRU
Paris
Marne
DÉLICE DE ST-CYR
Dreux
Versailles
COULOMMIERS
FEUILLE DE DREUX
Orly
see page 54
Rambouillet
Eure
Seine
Melun
BRIE DE MELUN
Chartres
Fontainebleau
BRIE DE MONTEREAU
Etampes
FONTAINEBLEAU
see page 45
Nemours
see page 24

## *Cheeses* Cow's milk

**Brie** soft, white rind, the size of a long-playing record. It will be frequently described with the addition of the name of the area in which it is made: **Brie de Coulommiers**; **Brie de Meaux**; **Brie de Melun**; and **Brie de Montereau** are the best known. Faint mushroom smell
**Chevru** similar in size and taste to Brie de Meaux
**Coulommiers** like Brie, but a smaller, 45 rpm disc. At its best in summer, autumn and winter. Both cheeses are ideal with **Côte de Beaune** reds
**Délice de Saint Cyr** a soft, triple-cream cheese – nutty-tasting and made in small disks
**Explorateur** a mild, triple-cream cheese – made in small cylinders
**Feuille de Dreux** fruity-flavoured, soft disk. Ideal with fruity red wines
**Fontainebleau** a fresh cream cheese with whipped cream; add a dusting of sugar – and it really is great

## *Regional Specialities*

Refer to the five regional lists elsewhere in *Bon Voyage*: Normandy to the west; the North; Champagne-Ardenne to the east; and Burgundy and the Loire on the southern borders of the Ile de France.

## *Wines*

Refer to the chapters of Champagne-Ardenne – to the east; and Burgundy and the Loire – to the south.

## *Books to take to France*

If you are visiting Paris, take the Michelin Green Guide to Paris – one of the very best tourist guides you'll ever use; and *The Food Lover's Guide to Paris*. The latter, written by Patricia Wells, is a classic reference book, with listings and descriptions of restaurants, cafés, *salons de thé, bistros à vin*, markets, pâtisseries, boulangeries, fromageries, charcuteries, chocolateries and much else besides. It's published in the UK by Methuen and in North America by Workman.

For the rest of France, the Michelin Green Guides provide invaluable information on the various regions covered by this book. There are 27 in total, but only eight are in English.

There is an extensive list of books, both general guides to France and more specific books on particular regions and subjects, in the *Guide for the Traveller in France*, available free from French Tourist Offices (addresses on page 47). The Tourist Offices will also supply further detailed literature on all the regions of France.

On the subject of food, I recommend *The Food Lover's Guide to France* by Patricia Wells (see above). In this book (also published by Methuen) the author extends her quest for good food to every region in France.

For information on the wines of France, the following are all old favourites:

*Bordeaux* David Peppercorn (Faber)
*Great Vineyards and Winemakers* Serena Sutcliffe (Macdonald)
*Guide to the Wines and Vineyards of France* Alexis Lichine (Papermac)
*Guide to Visiting Vineyards* Anthony Hogg (Michael Joseph)
*Vineyards and Vignerons* Robin and Judith Yapp (Yapp Bros, Mere, Wilts)
*The Wine Book* Jancis Robinson (A & C Black)
*Wine with Food* Derek Cooper (Marks & Spencer)

See also *Maps* under *Practical Information*, page 47.

# JURA

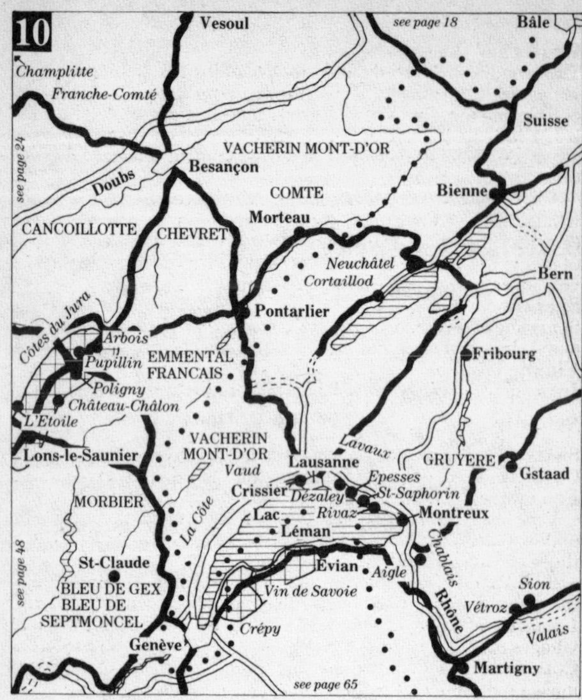


## *Cheeses* Cow's milk

**Cancoillotte** very fruity flavour, prepared from **Metton** (an unmoulded, recooked cheese) and looks like a cheese spread. It is available all through the year and is eaten warm in sandwiches or on slices of toast
**Comté** a hard, cooked cheese, made in great disks. Has holes the size of hazelnuts. Best seasons are summer, autumn and winter
**Emmental Français** – the French version; another hard, cooked cheese, also made in huge disks but with holes the size of walnuts
**Gex (Blue de)** a *fromage persillé*, with blue veins, like the pattern of parsley. Made in large disks; at its best in summer and autumn
**Morbier** strong-flavoured, pressed, uncooked thick disk
**Septmoncel (Bleu de)** made in thick disks – blue veins, slightly bitter
**Vacherin Mont-d'Or** soft, mild and creamy; made in cylinders

### Goat's milk

**Chevret** faint goat smell with this small flat disk or square-shaped cheese

## *Swiss Cheeses*

In Switzerland look out for the principal Swiss cheeses: the main types of **Emmental** and **Gruyère** have many varieties – all superb; others are **Vacherin Mont-d'Or**, **Tomme de Valbroye** and **Chèvre de Valois**

## *Regional Specialities*

**Brési** wafer-thin slices of dried beef
**Gougère** hot cheese pastry – based on Comté cheese
**Jésus de Morteau** fat sausage smoked over pine and juniper
**Poulet au vin jaune** chicken, cream and morilles, cooked in *vin jaune*

## *Wines*

**Whites and Rosés**
The broadest AC classification is **Côtes du Jura**. Among the best wines are the refreshing rosés from **Arbois**, brownish-pink in colour, and the whites of **Poligny**, fragrant and light. Another AC is **L'Etoile** (just north of Lons), where nice dry and sweet whites are made. There is also an **AC Arbois-Pupillin**, a small village to the south of Arbois.

The brightest star is a *vin jaune*, **AC Château-Châlon**, a rare wine, deep yellow, very dry and made from the Savagnin (Traminer) grape. **L'Etoile** and **Arbois** have their own versions of this *vin jaune*. A *vin de paille* (grapes dried on straw mats) is a very sweet, heady wine; *vin gris* is a pale rosé.

**Sparkling wines**
Sparkling wines include **L'Etoile mousseux**, the **Côtes du Jura** and **Arbois mousseux** and the *vin fou* (mad wine) from **Arbois**.

**Vins de Pays**
**Jura** and **Franche-Comté** labels (**Champlitte** is a village).

## *Swiss Wines*

Swiss wines are known by grape, place and type names. Chasselas is the main white grape: in **Valais** it's used to make **Fendant**; in **Vaud** it's **Dorin**; around Geneva **Perlan**.

Very little red wine is produced: it's made from the Pinot Noir and/or Gamay grape types. The reds of Valais are called **Dôle**; those of Vaud are named **Salvagnin**.

Fine Valais wines come from **Sion**, **Vétroz** and – best of all – the **Domaine du Mont d'Or**. The best Vaud wines are from **Lavaux** (between Lausanne and Montreux) and its principal villages of **Dézaley**, **Rivaz**, **Epesses**, **St-Saphorin** and **Aigle**; **La Côte** (Vaud) is the area south-west of Lausanne. **Neuchâtel** makes reds and whites (best village – **Cortaillod**).

# LANGUEDOC-ROUSSILLON

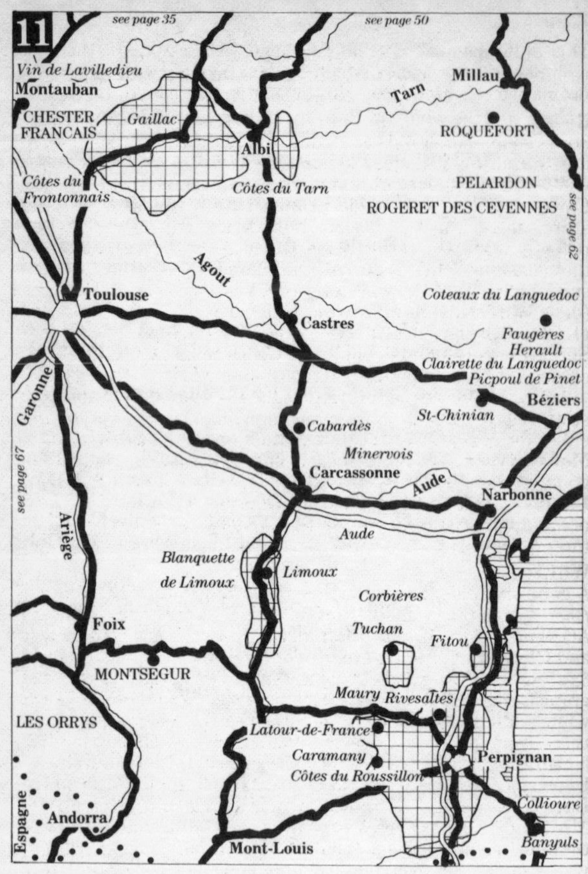


## *Cheeses* Cow's milk

**Chester Français** French Cheshire cheese from Castres and Gaillac
**Montségur** bland, pressed and uncooked disk
**Les Orrys** strong-flavoured – big disk; drink with fruity **Corbières**

### Goat's milk

**Pélardon** a *generic* name; small disks, nutty-tasting and soft. **Rogeret des Cévennes** is a related cheese

## *Regional Specialities*

**Aïgo Bouido** garlic soup. A marvellous, aromatic dish; the garlic is boiled, so its impact is lessened. Served with bread
**Boles de picoulat** small balls of chopped-up beef and pork, garlic and eggs – served with tomatoes and parsley
**Bouillinade** a type of *bouillabaisse* – with potatoes, oil, garlic and onions
**Boutifare** a sausage-shaped pudding of bacon and herbs
**Cargolade** snails, stewed in wine
**Millas** cornmeal porridge
**Ouillade** a heavy soup of bacon, *boutifare*, leeks, carrots and potatoes
**Touron** a pastry of almonds, green pistachio nuts, hazelnuts and fruit

*Wines*

This is the land of *Vins de Pays* and *Vin Ordinaire*: the vast majority of table wines which French people drink with their ordinary meals come from this huge area of the Midi.

**Reds**

Some good, strong reds are made: **Côtes du Roussillon**, **Côtes du Roussillon Villages** (25 villages share this AC – they make wines with a higher alcohol content and yield less wine per acre), **Caramany** and **Latour-de-France** (these two villages also share the general AC but can show their own names) have all recently won AC classifications. Other AC wines are **Fitou** (on the coast and the same AC is shared by the countryside surrounding Tuchan) and **Collioure**. VDQS reds are **Minervois** (dry), **Vin Noble du Minervois**, **Cabardès**, **Côtes du Cabardès et de l'Orbiel**, **Corbières** (soft and fruity), **Corbières Supérieures** (higher alcohol) and **Costières du Gard** (see map on page 62); some whites and rosés are made in all these areas.

A vast VDQS area to the north is the **Coteaux du Languedoc**; scattered throughout it are many individual *communes*, taking either the general classification or their own VDQS. **St-Chinian**, **Montpeyroux**, **Faugères** and **St-Saturnin** are four particularly good wines: other villages are **Cabrières**, **la Clape**, **Pic-Saint-Loup**, **Quatourze**, **St-Drézéry**, **St-Georges-d'Orques** (just west of Montpellier), **La Méjanelle**, **St-Christol** and **Vérargues** (last three have **Coteaux de** with village name).

**Whites**

A good, inexpensive, sparkling white is **Blanquette de Limoux** *(méthode champenoise)*: **Limoux nature** is still wine. These are AC wines as are **Vin de Blanquette**, **Clairette du Languedoc** and **Clairette de Bellegarde** (east of Nîmes – see map on page 62): the last two get their name from the Clairette grape; this grape is the traditional one for many French vermouths. A VDQS white is **Picpoul de Pinet** (Picpoul is the Armagnac grape). A *vin vert* – from the Roussillon – is a light, refreshing white wine.

**Natural Sweet Wines (Vins Doux Naturels) Liqueur Wines**

Unusual AC wines to look out for are the rich, golden **Muscats** of **Lunel**, **Rivesaltes**, **Frontignan**, **Mireval** and **St-Jean-de-Minervois**; fortified wines, rich in sugar and with added alcohol – they are ideal *apéritifs* (made from Muscat grapes). Similar wines, but darker in colour, like port, and made principally from the Grenache and Malvoisie grapes, are **Banyuls**, **Banyuls Grand Cru**, **Maury**, **Rivesaltes**, **Frontignan** and **Grand Roussillon** (the general AC for the VDN wines of the area). Those kept for a long time are called **Rancio**.

**Other wines**

Far to the north-west (and certainly not classified as Languedoc wines) are those from the **Gaillac** area – see page 36.

**Vins de Pays**

Most of it is red and much of it is good wine. If you see it called **Vin de Pays d'Oc** it will have come from any part of the four *départements* that follow. It may on the other hand indicate just the *département* name: **Vin de Pays des Pyrénées-Orientales** or **de l'Aude** or **de l'Hérault** or **du Gard**. Or the label may show a small, specific area within those *départements* (there are more than 50). Space does not provide the chance to list them all but a few are worth a mention: **Coteaux de Peyriac** (from the Minervois); **Haute Vallée de l'Orb** (north of St-Chinian); **Haute Vallée de l'Aude** (Limoux); **Les Sables du Golfe du Lion** (page 62); **Pays Catalan**, **Côte Catalane**, **Val d'Agly** (Roussillon).

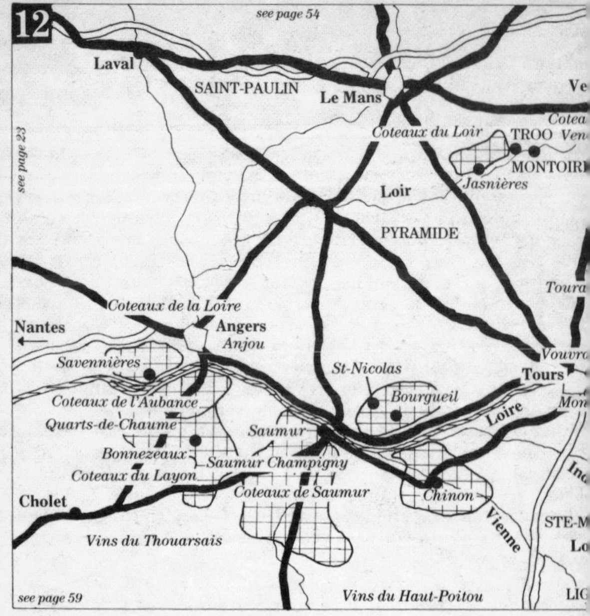


## *Cheeses* Cow's milk

**Olivet Bleu** small disk, often wrapped in leaves. A fruity taste and a light scent of blue mould. Try it with a red **Bourgueil**

**Olivet Cendré** savory taste. Cured in wood ashes. Same size as Olivet Bleu. **Chinon** is the wine to drink with it. **Gien** is a related cheese

**Frinault** a soft, small disk – ideal with light Loire wines

**Pithiviers au Foin** also known as **Bondaroy au Foin**. A soft cheese, made in thin disks and protected by a covering of bits of hay

**Saint-Benoit** a fruity, soft, small disk

**Saint-Paulin** semi-hard, yellow, mild, smooth-textured with a washed, bright orange rind. Made commercially throughout northern France

**Vendôme Bleu (Vendôme Cendré)** related to the Olivet cheeses. Not many seen these days in shops

Make sure you try some of the delightful fresh cream cheeses called **crémets**, eaten with sugar and fresh cream – delicious!

### Goat's milk

**Crottin de Chavignol** from the area just west of **Sancerre**, which, with **Chavignol**, makes the ideal wine to accompany it. It takes the form of a small, flattened ball. In grilled form it now appears regularly throughout France as a hot cheese course. The best season is winter. (Please also refer to the cheeses listed in the Berry-Bourbonnais region)

**Levroux** identical to Valençay. Nutty flavour

**Ste-Maure** summer and autumn season. Soft cylinders, full goat flavour cheese. Try it with dry **Vouvray** and **Montlouis** wines or the reds of **Chinon** and **Bourgueil**. **Ligueil** is a similar related cheese

**Selles-sur-Cher** from the Sologne; also known as **Romorantin**. Dark blue skin, pure white interior with mild, nutty flavour. **Montoire** and **Troo** (the home of Jane Grigson) are related cheeses

**Valençay** pyramid shaped, usual best seasons for all goat's milk cheeses – summer and autumn. Mild, soft and nutty taste. Often called **Pyramide**

## *Regional Specialities*

**Alose à l'oseille** grilled shad with a sorrel sauce
**Bardette** stuffed cabbage
**Beuchelle à la Tourangelle** kidneys, sweetbreads, morels, truffles, cream
**Bourdaines** apples stuffed with jam and baked
**Crémets** fresh cream cheese, eaten with sugar and cream
**Sandre** freshwater fish, like perch
**Truffiat** potato cake

## *Wines*

**Whites** *best years* **78 79 81 82 83 85**
All the Loire wines are charming, light and quite dissimilar in character from each other. The various **Muscadet** wines, which I let Brittany claim as its own, are white, dry and fruity.

White wines from the huge wine-producing areas of **Anjou** and **Touraine** can be sweet, medium-sweet or dry (check wine lists carefully – refer to the terms on page 26). Amongst the many whites worth recording is a personal favourite, **Vouvray**, made just east of Tours from the Chenin Blanc grape, the most important of the Loire white grape types; it is a particularly delicate wine. South of Angers is the **Coteaux du Layon**, with its own very broad AC. Here some fine sweet whites are made: **Quarts-de-Chaume**, **Coteaux du Layon Chaume** and **Bonnezeaux** (all three are sweet) have their own appellations. **Savennières** (dry whites), near Angers, lies on the north bank of the Loire: within that tiny area is **Savennières-Roches-aux-Moines** and **Savennières-Coulée-de-Serrant**, both small vineyards and both making magnificent dry wines.

Look out for the medium-sweet whites of **Jasnieres**, from the **Coteaux du Loir**, to the north of Tours; good-value wines of all shades are made here. In the neighbourhood of Tours, the Sauvignon grape is used for a **Sauvignon de Touraine** wine; a much cheaper alternative to Sancerre and nearly equal in quality. A **Touraine Azay-le-Rideau** (Chenin Blanc grape again) is a super dry white. Dry and semi-sweet wines are **Saumur**, **Coteaux de Saumur**, **Coteaux de l'Aubance** and **Anjou Coteaux de la Loire**.

**Sparkling Wines** *best years* **as above**

Particularly good are all the dry, sparkling wines; *mousseux* and *pétillant*. The **Vouvray** *sec* and *demi-sec pétillant* whites are superb; others to enjoy are **Montlouis**, just across the river from Vouvray, **Anjou**, **Touraine**, **Saumur** (these, too, are really good) and a delicious **Crémant de Loire**. All these sparkling wines are moreish wines; it is much too easy to empty the bottle.

**Other Whites** *best years* **78 79 81 82 83 85**

From the Upper Loire, outside my region and to the east, come some lovely white wines, made from the Sauvignon Blanc grape: **Pouilly-Fumé** and **Sancerre**, both flinty and smoky flavoured. Another white is **Quincy**, from an area south of Vierzon, dryer than Fumé. **Pouilly-sur-Loire** wines are from the same general area, but the wines are inferior, being made from a different grape type, Chasselas. An unknown AC is **Menetou-Salon**, just north of Bourges; it makes dry wines of all shades. **Reuilly**, **Valençay** and **Cheverny** wines are dry and fragrant (they make all shades). The last four named whites, all excellent, are produced from the Sauvignon grape. The same grape is used in the VDQS **Coteaux du Giennois** and **Côtes de Gien** whites.

**Rosés** *best years* **47 49 55 59 69 71 75 76 78 81 82**

There are some notable rosés from **Saumur** and **Anjou** – and their respective **Coteaux** – from **Touraine**, **Touraine Mesland**, **Touraine Amboise** and from the **Coteaux de l'Aubance**, on the south bank of the Loire, opposite Angers. Look out for **Rosé d'Anjou**, **Rosé de Loire** and a rosé made from two different grape types, **Cabernet d'Anjou** (Cabernets Franc and Sauvignon). The **Cabernet de Saumur** is lighter in colour and dryer than the Anjou wine. There is also a sparkling **Rosé d'Anjou pétillant**. From the Sancerre area come good rosés; often described on wine lists as **Rosé de Bué** and **Rosé de Chavignol**. VDQS rosés are the **Coteaux du Vendômois** and **Vins de l'Orléanais** (a *vin gris* – light, pale and fragrant).

**Reds** *best years* **as above**

Amongst the good Loire Cabernet reds are **Chinon**, **Bourgueil**, **Saint-Nicolas-de-Bourgueil**, **Anjou** and **Saumur-Champigny**. **Sancerre** produces a small amount of excellent red wine, made from the Pinot Noir grape. A **Gamay de Touraine** is a red made from the same grape type used in Beaujolais; other Gamay wines are **Anjou Gamay**, **Cheverny**, **Valençay** and **Coteaux d' Ancenis** (page 49). The VDQS **Vins du Thouarsais** are sound reds; wines of all shades share this classification. Remember Angers is the home of **Cointreau**.

**Vins de Pays**

These will have labels showing either the *département* or the general area name; examples are **Vin de Pays de Loir-et-Cher** or, in the second case, a **Vin de Pays du Jardin de la France**. Often the labels will also describe the grape type: Sauvignon (Blanc); Chenin Blanc; and Gamay are examples. Some of these Fourth Division wines really do compare well with their First Division brothers. Try them – and surprise yourself.

Refer also to the chapters on Brittany (see page 22) and Berry-Bourbonnais (see page 20) for other wines.

## Practical Information

*Telephones*

*Making phone calls within France*

If you ring ahead to any hotel or restaurant, always remember to dial **16** (the French internal code) before you continue with the area code. If you are making a call from the same area as the area code then it is only necessary to ring the number of the establishment – you must **not** dial 16 or the area code.

*Making phone calls to other countries*

If you ring abroad, dial **19** first to obtain an overseas line but then **wait** until you hear a continuous tone before dialling the country code you need. (For UK calls: always drop 0 from the STD code you are ringing.)

*Phonecards*

Many telephone booths take a phonecard or *télécarte*, available from post offices or where shown on telephone booths.

*Maps*

For finding your way in Paris, the Michelin *Paris Atlas* (No 11) is pocket-sized and practical. For negotiating the périphérique ring road, the Automobile Association publishes the large scale *AA Paris Ring Road Map*, which shows link roads and junction exit sign information.

The *AA Road Map France* covers the whole country at a scale of 1 cm to 10 km. For particular areas, I recommend you use the Michelin yellow regional maps of France in the 200 numbered series (230–46), and the yellow detailed maps numbered 51–90. Both are in the scale of 1 cm to 2 km, and are good for large-scale touring. Also useful are the Institut Géographique National (IGN) *série verte* maps (scale 1 cm to 1 km), which are local maps showing footpaths, and the *série rouge* maps (scale 1 cm to 2.5 km) which cover the regions and are for drivers, showing places of particular tourist or cultural interest.

Make use of the annual *Bison Futé* (Clever Buffalo) map published by the French Ministry of Transport. It shows traffic-free, bypass routes throughout France and is available, free of charge, from large garages in France or from AA port offices in the UK.

*French Tourist Offices*

When in France, get used to asking for advice at the local tourist offices – Offices de Tourisme and *Syndicats d'Initiative* – which can advise on accommodation, restaurants, and transport. The following French Tourist Offices are useful sources of information before you go:

**London** W1V 0AL, 178 Piccadilly
**New York** (N.Y. 10020), 610 Fifth Avenue
**Chicago** (Illinois 60611), 645 North Michigan Av – Suite 430
**Dallas** (Texas 75258), World Trade Center 103, 2050 Stemmons Freeway, P.O. Box 58610
**Beverly Hills** (Cal. 90212), 9401 Wilshire Boul
**Montréal** (P.Q. H3H 1E 4), 1840 Ouest, Rue Sherbrooke
**Toronto** (M5H 2W9 Ont.) 372 Bay St – Suite 610

See also *Times and Holidays*, page 57.

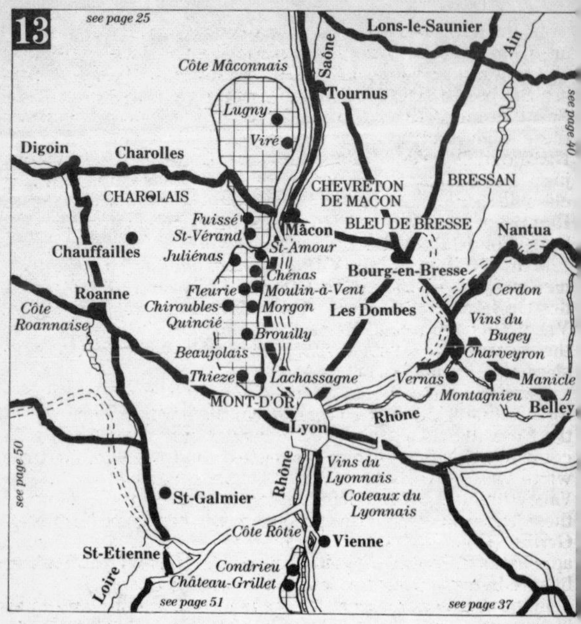


## *Cheeses* Cow's milk

**Bresse (Bleu de)** available all the year. A mild, soft, blue cheese, made in small cylinders. Ideal with **Beaujolais** wines
**Mont-d'Or** from just north of Lyon. Small disks – delicate, savory taste

### Goat's milk

**Bressan** a small, truncated cone – also known as **Petit Bressan**
**Charolais (Charolles)** soft, nutty-flavoured, small cylinder
**Chevreton de Mâcon** if made of pure goat's milk it is at its best in summer and autumn. A light blue rind and slightly nutty taste
Without fail try **fromage blanc**; a fresh cream cheese, eaten with sugar and fresh cream – if you've never tried some, you've missed something

## *Regional Specialities*

**Bresse (Poulet, Poularde, Volaille de)** the best French poultry. Fed on corn and, when killed, bathed in milk. Flesh is white and delicate
**Gras-double** ox tripe, served with onions
**Poulet demi-deuil** *half-mourning*; called this because of the thin slices of truffle placed underneath the chicken breast; cooked in a *court-bouillon*
**Poulet au vinaigre** chicken, shallots, tomatoes, white wine, wine vinegar and a cream sauce
**Rosette** a large pork sausage
**Tablier de sapeur** *gras-double* coated with flour, egg-yolk, breadcrumbs

## *Wines*

In Lyon they say there are three rivers: the Rhône, the Saône and the Beaujolais! For my taste some of the most enjoyable red wine comes from this part of France, much of it being inexpensive, even if you choose it at the greatest restaurants. I cannot stress this last piece of information enough; local wines are not prohibitively expensive, even at the region's three star places.

All the reds come from the Gamay grape type. The best wines are from the *communes* of **Moulin-à-Vent**, **Brouilly**, **Fleurie** and **Morgon**; for some, like myself, the **Côte de Brouilly** wines are the best of all. Other notable *communes* are **Chiroubles**, **Saint Amour**, **Chénas** and **Juliénas**. Wines not coming from these nine specific areas are either bottled under the **AC Beaujolais**, **AC Beaujolais Supérieur** (not superior in quality, just more alcohol strength) or **AC Beaujolais-Villages** classifications (see below). Near Roanne, look out for a good **Renaison** rosé and **Côte Roannaise** reds (fine with *Charolais* beef). For details of **Côte Mâconnais** wines see page 27.

Many **AC Beaujolais Villages** wines will give their village names: **Quincié**, **Lancié**, **St-Etienne-la-Varenne**, **St-Etienne-des-Oullières**, **St-Lager**, **Romanèche-Thorins**, **Beaujeu**, **Vaux**, **Charentay** and **Regnié** are examples. Other villages, in the south of Beaujolais territory, like **Lachassagne** and **Theizé** share the general Beaujolais AC.

South of Lyon is the start of the **Côtes du Rhône**. Lyon claims for itself the **Côte Rôtie** (wines from the northernmost part of the Côtes du Rhône, south of Vienne). Some magnificent reds come from the Rôtie – it means *roasted* – but two world-famous white wines are also made in this narrow part of the Rhône Valley; both come from the rare Viognier grape. Tiny amounts of these expensive wines are produced: **Condrieu** and **Château-Grillet** (from a 3½ acre vineyard, one of the smallest French appellations). **Vins du Lyonnais** and **Coteaux du Lyonnais** are light reds, made from the Gamay and Syrah grape types.

In the south-east corner of the region you will find some good, inexpensive, and not well-known Bressan wines, **Vins du Bugey**: these are the whites of **Montagnieu** and **Manicle** and the reds of **Charveyron** and **Vernas**. Manicle – the name of the grape type – comes from an area 10 km north-west of Belley. **Cerdon** or **Bugey pétillant** and **mousseux** are sparkling wines. Other wines from the Belley area are **Roussette de Virieu** and **Roussette du Bugey**. You may also see a **Cerdon rosé**.

# MASSIF CENTRAL

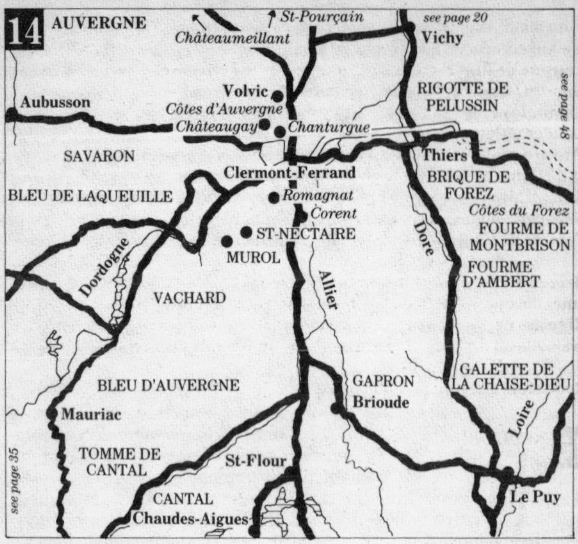

14
AUVERGNE
St-Pourçain
Châteaumeillant
see page 20
Vichy
Volvic
Côtes d'Auvergne
Aubusson
Châteaugay
Chanturgue
RIGOTTE DE
PELUSSIN
see page 48
SAVARON
Thiers
Clermont-Ferrand
BRIQUE DE
FOREZ
BLEU DE LAQUEUILLE
Romagnat
Corent
Côtes du Forez
ST-NECTAIRE
FOURME DE
MONTBRISON
MUROL
Dordogne
Dore
FOURME
D'AMBERT
VACHARD
Allier
GALETTE DE
LA CHAISE-DIEU
BLEU D'AUVERGNE
GAPRON
Brioude
Mauriac
Loire
TOMME DE
CANTAL
St-Flour
see page 35
CANTAL
Le Puy
Chaudes-Aigues

## *Cheeses* Cow's milk

**Auvergne (Bleu d')** when made on farms at its best in summer and autumn. Strong smell, soft, made in the same way as Roquefort. **Bleu de Laqueuille** is a related cheese

**Cantal** from the Auvergne. Semi-hard, nutty flavour. Praised by Pliny. Try it with the fruity **Côtes d'Auvergne** reds

**Causses (Bleu des)** a blue cheese with parsley-like veins, hence the term *persillé*. At its best in summer and autumn

16
CEVENNES
Chaudes-Aigues
Allier
LAGUIOLE
Lot
Mende
see page 35
BLEU DES
CAUSSES
Vin de Marcillac
Rodez
Aveyron
see page 62
Rouergue
Tarn
Florac
Gard
Alès
Millau
Le Vigan
Albi
ROQUEFORT
Montpeyroux
Aniane
Côtes du Tarn
see page 42
St-Saturnin
Gignac

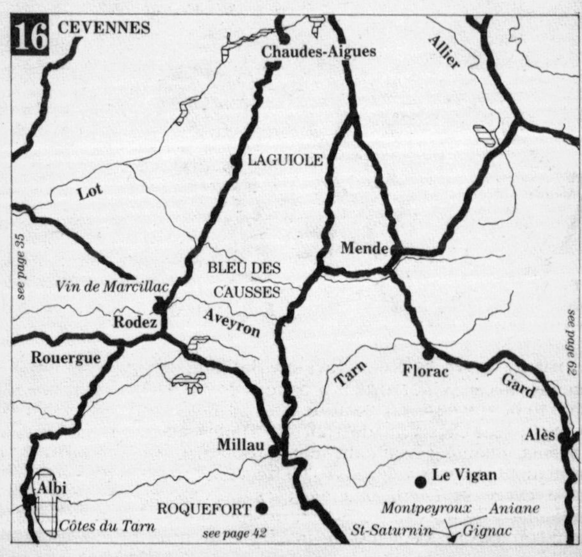

**Fourme-d'Ambert** has a summer and autumn season. A blue cheese from the Auvergne and in the shape of a tall cylinder
**Fourme de Montbrison** a bitter blue – as is **Fourme de Pierre-s-Haute**
**Gapron (Gaperon)** a garlic-flavoured, flattened ball
**Laguiole** related to Cantal. Big cylinders, penetrating bouquet
**Loudes (Bleu de)** blue-veined and from the hills of Velay, near Le Puy
**Murol** a semi-hard cheese, like St-Nectaire. Made in small disks, mild
**St-Félicien** a salty-tasting cheese from the hills west of Tournon
**St-Nectaire** has a purply-brown skin, made in larger disks than Murol. A semi-hard, mild cheese. **Savaron** and **Vachard** are related
**Tomme de Cantal** a fresh, softish, cream-coloured, unfermented cheese

## Goat's milk

**Brique du Forez** also known as **Chevreton d'Ambert**. A small loaf with a nutty flavour. **Galette de la Chaise-Dieu** is similar – a flat cake
**Rigotte de Condrieu** soft, small cylinders with no special flavour; available all the year. **Rigotte de Pelussin** is a related cheese

## Ewe's milk

**Roquefort** read the notes below

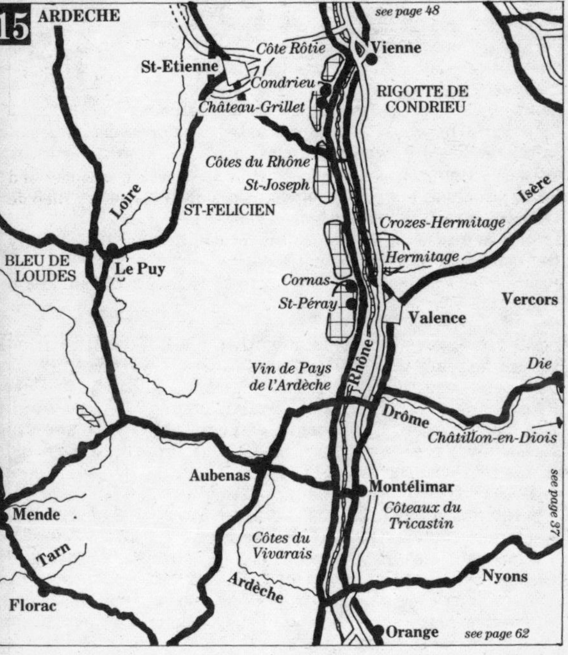


Visit the town of **Roquefort-sur-Soulzon** where the most famous cheese in the world is produced. Inspect the many caves (said to be the best refrigeration sites in the world) where this exquisite blue cheese, made from ewe's milk, is stored and where it ripens, emerging eventually into that sharp, fine taste enjoyed throughout the world. Over 15,000 tonnes of these cheeses are made every year. All blue cheeses are salty – Roquefort particularly so – as salt is added to slow down the growth of mould on the outside, while the inside matures.

## *Regional Specialities*

**Aligot** purée of potatoes with Tomme de Cantal cheese, cream, garlic and butter
**Bougnette** a stuffing of pork, bread and eggs – wrapped in *crépine* (caul)
**Bourriols d'Aurillac** sweet pancakes, made from buckwheat flour
**Brayaude (gigot)** lamb cooked in white wine, onions and herbs
**Cadet Mathieu** pastry turnover filled with slices of apple
**Clafoutis** baked pancake batter, poured over fruit, usually cherries
**Confidou Rouergat** ragout of beef, red wine, tomatoes, garlic and onions
**Cousinat (Cousina)** chestnut soup (*salée* – salted) with cream, butter and prunes – served with bread
**Criques** grated potato, mixed with eggs and fried – in the form of pancakes. Related to the *Truffiat* of Berry
**Farçon** large *galette* of sausage, sorrel, onions, eggs and white wine
**Farinette** buckwheat flour pancakes – meat and vegetable filling
**Friand Sanflorin** pork meat and herbs in pastry
**Jambon d'Auvergne** a lovely mountain ham
**Manouls** see *Trénels*
**Milliard (Millat, Milla)** see *Clafoutis*
**Mourtayrol** a stew with beef, chicken, ham, vegetables and bread
**Omelette Brayaude** eggs, pork, cheese and potatoes
**Perdrix à l'Auvergnate** partridge stewed in white wine
**Potée Auvergnate** stew of vegetables, cabbage, pork and sausage
**Pountari** a mince of pork fat in cabbage leaves
**Pounti** small, egg-based savoury soufflé with bacon or prunes
**Rouergat(e)** Rouergue; the name of the area to the west of Millau
**Salmis de colvert Cévenole** wild duck, sautéed in red wine, onions, ham and mushrooms
**Soupe aux choux** soup with cabbage, ham, pork, bacon and turnips
**Trénels** mutton tripe, white wine and tomatoes
**Tripoux** stuffed sheep's feet
**Truffade** a huge *galette* of sautéed potatoes

## *Wines*

For those visitors based in the northern part of the Massif, look out for the really good **St-Pourçain** (near Vichy) reds and a fine Loire-type white wine. A flourishing VDQS area is **Côtes d'Auvergne**, near Clermont-Ferrand: among the noteworthy reds from here are **Chanturgue** and **Châteaugay** – made from the Gamay grape – and a rosé from **Corent**. From the eastern side of this northern section of the Massif Central come some good Beaujolais-type reds, the Gamays of the **Côtes du Forez**.

If you are in the Tain area you are in the middle of one of the best wine-producing parts of France. From Tain l'Hermitage (AC **Hermitage**, a wonderful wine and **AC Crozes-Hermitage**, a less-good, junior brother), **Saint Joseph** and **Cornas**, all north of Valence and on both sides of the Rhône, you will find some super ruby-red wines, dark and powerful. Only the vineyards on the granite hill overlooking Tain have the right to the world-famous Hermitage appellation; the vineyards that lie to the north and east take the Crozes AC.

There are also some good, dry whites from this area: a **Hermitage Blanc** (the best one is **Chante-Alouette**), a **Saint Péray** white and a **Crozes-Hermitage** one. The highlight of the area for me is the **Saint Péray mousseux** – sheer delight! 80 per cent of the vineyard production goes towards the making of this sparkling wine – manufactured in the same way as Champagne – *méthode champenoise*.

South-east of Valence, at **Die**, you will find the lovely *demi-se*

**Clairette de Die** (local, *naturel* method) and a *brut* version (*méthode champenoise*), both **mousseux**. There's a dry still white, too. Near Die are the wines of all shades from **Châtillon-en-Diois**. South of Valence is the **AC Coteaux du Tricastin** with dry rosés and reds. A century ago they were highly thought of; their prestige diminished – but in the last 20 years they have risen from a *Vins de Pays* classification to a full AC.

If you are in Millau, or anywhere in the south, look at my wine notes on pages 36 and 43. You may be offered many of the VDQS Midi wines (from Languedoc to the south): **Saint Chinian**, **Saint Saturnin**, **Montpeyroux** and **Faugères** are among the best. Other wines you will see on wine lists are the **Gaillac** ones – reds, rosés and whites (both still and sparkling). You may also come across the light reds from just west and north of Rodez, the VDQS **Vin de Marcillac**. Try this local wine with a Fourme-d'Ambert cheese.

**Vins de Pays**

The **Vin de Pays de l'Ardèche** reds (both Gamay and Syrah grapes) are superb examples of how good this classification of wines can be.

## *Tears of Glory*

During 1983 I was sent a small book by one of my readers, Simon Longe, who had read *France à la Carte* and *Hidden France* and knew of my great interest in the French Resistance. The paperback cost a modest £1.25 and I had not seen it before; I read the entire book within hours of receiving it! Like Simon, all my readers will know that I refer often to the heroic struggles of the Resistance; certainly whenever I write about the Vercors (see the eastern side of the Ardèche map) I am always reminded of the tragic events that occurred in those wooded mountains during the summer of 1944.

The book – published by Macmillan and Pan (paper) – is called *Tears of Glory*, and is available from libraries (it is out of print); it's by Michael Pearson and tells the true story of 'The Betrayal of Vercors 1944'. It is a riveting, heart-stirring story. When you know the geography of a place like the Vercors as intimately as I do, a book like this becomes a series of visual pictures as you turn each page. An added interest is that Simon's father, Desmond Longe, and his godfather, John Houseman, both played a part in the story of those tragic few months.

The Vercors merits the time and attention of every visitor to France. I implore you – find the time for this natural fortress, full of the majestic handiwork of Mother Nature at her most ferocious and spectacular. Read the splendid story before you go: I think it is the most watertight promise I have made in any of my books when I say that you will be enthralled by both the book and your on-the-spot visit. It will be an important addition to your understanding of people, modern history and geography. There is much to see.

I can think of no better way of motivating you to make a personal contribution towards repairing the broken bridges of the *Entente Cordiale*. You will not be disappointed.

*Thou that comest here*
*Bring thy soul with thee*

The words on the Grotte de la Luire memorial.

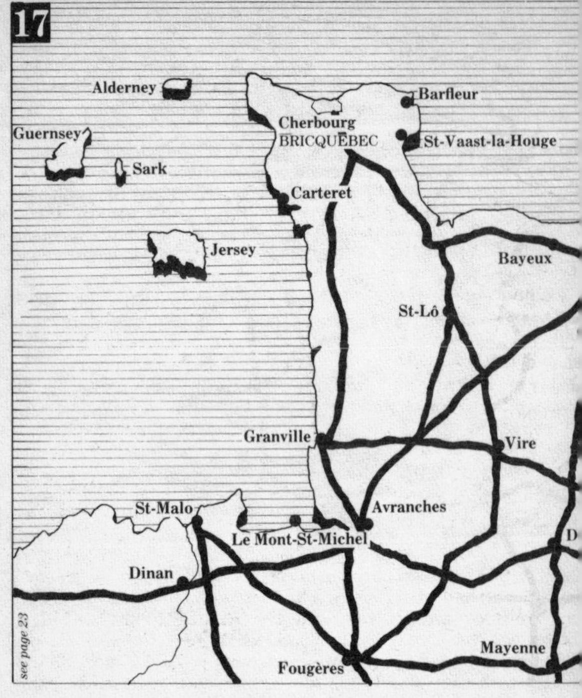


## *Cheeses* Cow's milk

**Bondon** (also called **Neufchâtel**) from Pays de Bray (north-east of Rouen). Small cylinder, soft and smooth. **Bondard** is related
**La Bouille** red-speckled, white rind; strong smell, fruity-tasting small disk
**Bricquebec** made by monks at the abbey of the same name. A mild-tasting, flat pressed disk. Available all the year
**Brillat-Savarin** mild, creamy disk – a triple-cream cheese. **Magnum** is the same cheese but much older
**Camembert** soft, milky flavour with a white rind, made as a small, flat disk. Available all the year and super with a **Beaujolais** wine
**Carré de Bray** small, square-shaped, mushroom-smelling cheese
**Cœur de Bray** fruity-tasting, heart-shaped cheese. Best in summer
**Demi-sel** mild, fresh and salted – made as a small square
**Excelsior** best in summer and autumn. Small cylinder, mild and soft
**Gournay** a one inch thick disk – slightly salty, soft and smooth
**Livarot** best in autumn and winter. Semi-hard, strong and gold. Spicy flavour – try it with a **Riesling**. **Mignot** is similar
**Monsieur** soft, fruity cylinder – strong smell
**Pavé d'Auge (Pavé de Moyaux)** spicy-flavoured, soft cheese, made in a yellow square. Try it with full-bodied reds
**Petit-Suisse** available all the year; a small, round, fresh cream cheese
**Pont-l'Evêque** rectangular or square shape, strong, soft and gold, at its best in summer, autumn and winter. First made in 13th-century

## *Regional Specialities*

**Andouillette de Vire** chitterling (tripe) sausage
**Barbue au cidre** brill cooked in cider and Calvados

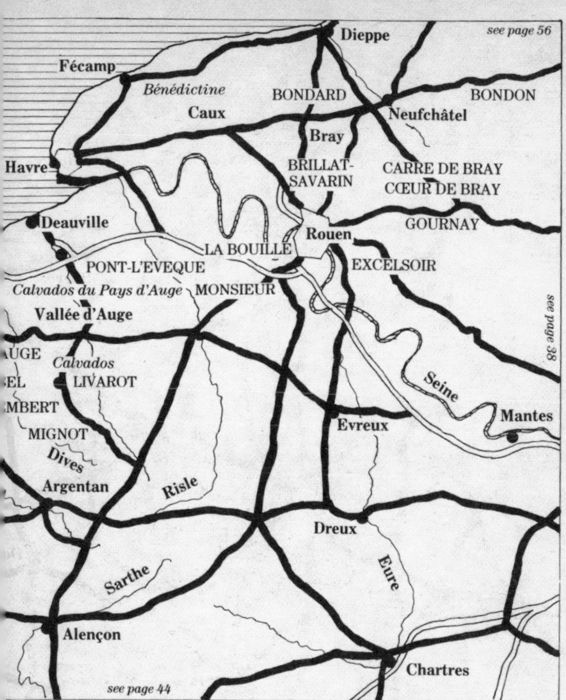


**auchoise (à la)** with cream, Calvados and apple

**ouillons de pommes à la Normande** apples in pastry and baked

**scalope (Vallée d'Auge)** veal sautéed, flamed in Calvados and served ith cream and apples

**icelle Normande** pancake with ham, mushrooms and cheese

**armite Dieppoise** a fish soup with some, or all of the following: sole, rbot, *rouget*, *moules*, *crevettes*, onions, white wine, butter and cream

**oulet (Vallée d'Auge)** chicken cooked in the same way as *escalope illée d'Auge*

**ipes à la mode de Caen** tripe – stewed, with onions, carrots, leeks, rlic, cider and Calvados

**rou Normand** Calvados – a 'dram', drunk in one gulp, between courses; stores the appetite

## *'ines*

here is nothing to say about wines in Normandy but, on the her hand, don't overlook the fact that **Bénédictine** is distilled Fécamp. And what better compensation could there be than **alvados**, another *digestive*; distilled apple brandy. There are no ss than 10 classified Calvados regions within Normandy but the est is the Appellation Contrôlée **Calvados du Pays d'Auge**. nis is a tightly specified area straddling the River Touques – the mous Vallée d'Auge country; see the list of regional specialities. nis particular Calvados must be distilled in stills known as *arentais* – there are two production stages. And – last but not ast – relish superb **cider**: *cidre bouché* – sparkling cider; *cidre ux* – sweet cider.

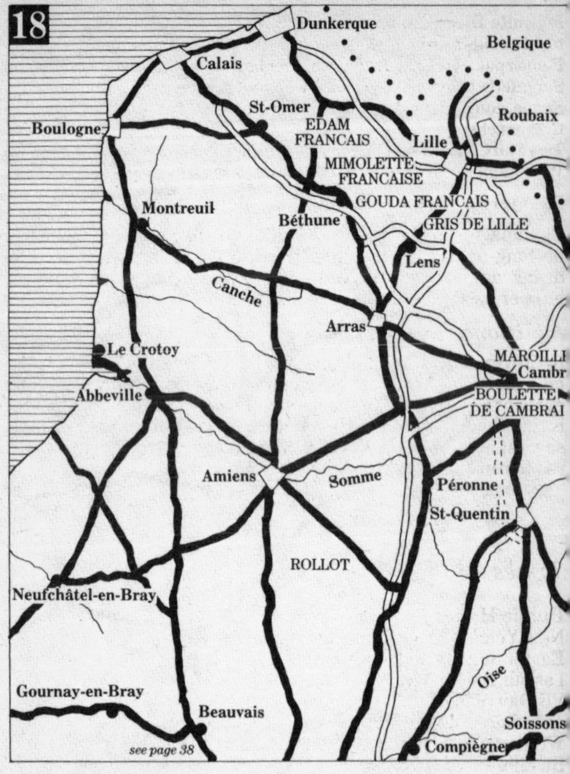


## *Cheeses* Cow's milk

**Boulette de Cambrai** a small, ball-shaped, soft, fresh cheese – flavoure with herbs. Available all the year

**Edam Français** a red ball without holes or with tiny ones

**Gouda Français** mild, yellow-coloured, small wheel

**Gris de Lille** a really salty square of cheese with a strong smell

**Maroilles** soft, slightly salty and gold. Appears in many regional dishes

**Mimolette Française** orange-coloured, ball-shaped cheese

**Rollot** spicy-tasting, soft, small yellow disk – sometimes heart-shaped

Be certain to visit Philippe Olivier's La Fromagerie at 43 Rue Thiers Boulogne; it's one of the best in the North

## *Regional Specialities*

**Carbonnade de bœuf à la Flamande** braised beef with beer, onions a bacon

**Caudière (Chaudière, Caudrée)** numerous versions of fish and pota soup served throughout the North

**Ficelle Normande** pancake with ham, mushrooms and cheese

**Flamiche aux Maroilles** see *Tarte aux Maroilles*

**Flamiche aux poireaux** puff-pastry tart with cream and leeks

**Gaufres** yeast waffles

**Goyère** see *Tarte aux Maroilles*

**Hochepot** a *pot-au-feu* of the North (see *Pepperpot*)

**Marmite Dieppoise** a fish soup with some, or all of the following: sole, turbot, *rouget*, *crevettes*, onions, white wine, butter and cream
**Pepperpot** stew of mutton, pork, beer and vegetables
**Sanguette** black pudding, made with rabbit's blood
**Soupe courquignoise** soup with white wine, fish, *moules*, leeks and Gruyère cheese
**Tarte aux Maroilles** a tart based on the local cheese (see Cheeses)
**Waterzooï** a cross between soup and stew, usually of fish or chicken

### *Wines*

Champagne to the east – Calvados to the south-west: there is nothing to talk about in the North other than **Genièvre**, a gin drunk as a liqueur, served chilled, and made from grain and juniper berries; and truly excellent beer.

### *Additional comments*

In previous editions of my books I have written that standards of cuisine in the North did not compare too favourably with other parts of France. One of the happier changes of the last few years is that things are looking up on the eating out front in the North – several new young chefs have brought a breath of fresh air to the restaurant scene.

## *Times and Holidays*

### Public Holidays

New Year's Day (1 January)
Easter Sunday and Monday
Labour Day (1 May)
VE Day (8 May)
Ascension Day (sixth Thursday after Easter)
Whitsun (seventh Sunday and Monday after Easter)
Bastille Day (14 July)
Assumption Day (15 August)
All Saints Day (1 November)
Remembrance Day (11 November)
Christmas Day (25 December)

### Shopping and business hours

**Banks** Open from 9am to 4pm on weekdays; closed for lunch. Closed on Sundays and either Saturday or Monday.
**Post offices** Open from 8am to 7pm on weekdays and on Saturday mornings until noon.
**Shops** are generally open until 6.30 or 7.30 in the evening (later for hypermarkets). Food shops often open at 7am, and on Sunday mornings. Many shops in small towns close for lunch, and shops are widely closed for all or part of Monday.

### Restaurants

Lunch starts at around noon, and the evening meal at around 7pm. Booking is advisable for Sunday lunchtimes; on Sunday evening many restaurants are closed.

### Summer Time

France is usually ahead of Britain. The clocks go forward on the last Sunday in March and go back on the last Sunday in September.

# POITOU-CHARENTES

*Cheeses* **Cow's milk**

**Jonchée** from Saintonge area. Fresh cream cheese – served with sugar and cream. **Caillebote** is a similar cheese

**Pigouille** small, creamy-flavoured disk – served on straw. Can also be made from goat's or ewe's milk

**Goat's milk**

**Chabichou** Poitou area cheese: *Laitier* (dairy made) and *Fermier* (farm made) – small, truncated, upright cylinders; soft, sharp-tasting cheese

**Couhé-Vérac** soft, nutty cheese made in small squares

**Jonchée** from Niort area. Mild, soft, creamy – best in summer and autumn. A cheese called **Lusignan** is similar, made as a disk

**La Mothe-St-Héray** best in summer and autumn. A small disk, one inch thick. Try it with the reds of **Haut-Poitou**. **Bougon** is a related cheese

**Pouligny-St-Pierre** pyramid-shaped; strong smell, soft cheese. A cheese called **Tournon-St-Pierre** is related

**Pyramide** pyramid-shaped, soft cheese

**Ruffec** fruity disk, made in a small disk

**Taupinière** packed and served in chestnut leaves

**Ewe's milk**

**Oléron** best in spring; mild, creamy, fresh cheese. Made on Ile d'Oléron; known also as **Jonchée d'Oléron** or **Brebis d'Oléron**

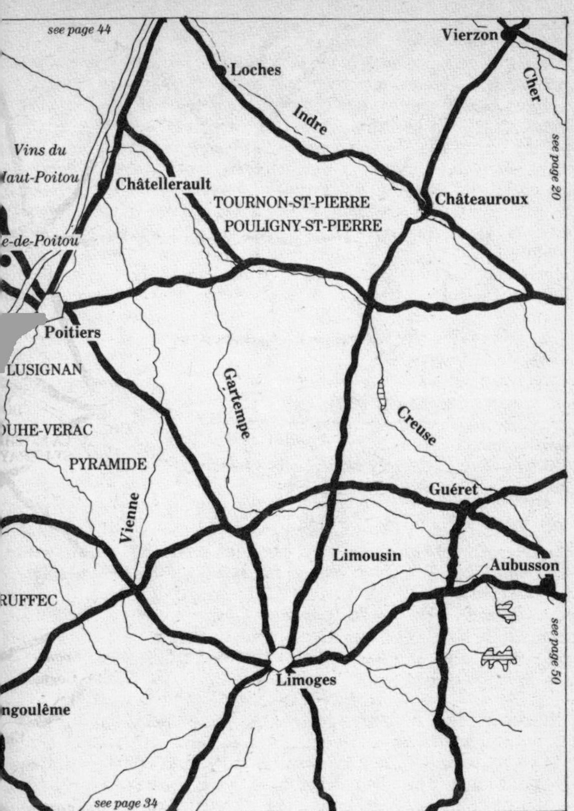


## Regional Specialities

**Bouilliture (Bouilleture)** a type of *matelote d'anguilles* – a freshwater eel stew in red wine, with shallots and prunes
**Boulaigou** thick sweet or savoury pancake
**Bréjaude** cabbage, leek and bacon soup
**Cagouilles** snails from the Charentes
**Casserons en matelote** squid in red wine sauce with garlic and shallots
**Cèpes** fine, delicate, flap mushrooms – don't miss them
**Chaudrée** a ragout of fish cooked in white wine, shallots and butter
**Chevrettes** local name for *crevettes* (shrimps)
**Clafoutis** pancake batter, poured over fruit (usually black cherries), and then baked – another treat you must not miss
**Embeurré de chou** white-heart cabbage, cooked in salted water, crushed and served with butter
**Farcidure** a dumpling – either poached or sautéed
**Farci Poitevin** a *pâté* of cabbage, spinach and sorrel, encased by cabbage leaves and cooked in a *bouillon*
**Migourée** a sort of *chaudrée*
**Mique** a stew of dumplings
**Mogette (Mojette)** small pulse beans in butter and cream
**Mouclade** mussels cooked in wine, egg yolks and cream; can be served

with some **Pineau des Charentes**
**Oysters** for an explanation of *les claires*, *belons*, *gravettes*, *marennes* and other terms see the paragraph that follows.

*Les Claires* are the oyster-fattening beds that you see in the local Marennes country. There are three types of **flat** oysters: *belons* (from the River Belon in Brittany) and *gravettes* (from Arcachon – south-west of Bordeaux) – these two are cultivated on their home ground; *marennes*, the third type, are transferred from Brittany and Arcachon to *les claires* where they finish their growth. **Dished** oysters (sometimes called *portugaises*) breed mainly in the Charente and Gironde Estuaries; these mature at Marennes. *Fines de claires* and *spéciales* are the largest – *huîtres de parc* are standard sized. All this lavish care covers a time span of between two to four years.

**Soupe aux fèves des Marais** soup of crushed broad beans with bread, sorrel, chevril and butter
**Soupe de moules à la Rochelaise** soup of various fish, mussels, saffron, garlic, tomatoes, onions and red wine
**Sourdons** cockles from the Charentes
**Tartisseaux** fritters
**Tourtou** thick buckwheat flour pancake

## *Wines*

The countryside of the Charentes offers the world its annual harvest of white grapes – a harvest that eventually matures into **Cognac**; brandy known as the finest on earth. The quality of Cognac varies with the fertility of the soil; this is why there are six districts. The best, **Grande Champagne**, is from the immediate south of Cognac town; the next four districts extend outwards to form a huge circle; the lowest classification is the coastal stretch lying alongside the Atlantic coast. Age is the other vital factor – the maturing process is all important. **Pineau des Charentes** is a liqueur wine (grape juice and Cognac); clear, sweet and heady – drink it cool as an *apéritif*.

Don't miss the chance to try some of the unknown locals of this part of France. The VDQS **Vins du Haut-Poitou** are a revelation: amongst them a **Sauvignon** white – just like its famous big brother from Sancerre; a **Pinot-Chardonnay** – the marvellous white grape of Burgundy; a **Gamay** red – best drunk cool; a dry rosé; and a dry, **Chenin** white. Some wine lists will describe the wines as **Poitou** or **Neuville de Poitou** – the main town of the wine-producing area.

**Vins de Pays**
Some really obscure wines will be recommended in the La Rochelle area: **Ile de Ré** and **Blanc de Ré** – dry whites from the Ile de Ré. You will also see a **Rosé de Mareuil** (a town in the Vendée); this is one of the wines, made in all shades, called **Vin de Pays de la Vendée** (the *département*) – also referred to by the marvellous name of **Fiefs Vendéens**.

# *Pen Pictures – some of the great names of French gastronomy*

**Jean-Anthelme Brillat-Savarin** (1755–1826) Born at Belley (see *Savoie*), he was the greatest of all French gastronomes. He was a lawyer by profession, a linguist, an inventor and violinist; a do-it-yourself publisher. His book *La Physiologie du goût* (published by Penguin as *The Philosopher in the Kitchen*) had a profound influence on gastronomic thinking.

**Antonin Carême** (1784–1833) By the end of the 18th century – during the French Revolution – *la grande cuisine* had ground to a halt. Carême, more than any other chef – through his writings and his genius for creating sauces – took it to new levels of excellence. The father of classical cuisine, he developed it to its extravagant excesses. He came from the poorest of families – one of 25 children. The first 'superstar' chef.

**Auguste Escoffier** (1847–1935) He became known as 'the King of chefs and the chef of kings'. Born at Villeneuve-Loubet (near Nice), he worked for over 40 years in various kitchens – mainly in London; he was one of the founders of the Savoy Hotel. Through his writings and his creative talent he had a great influence on classical cuisine; all modern masters of admit that they owe much to the sound principles laid down by Escoffier.

**Les Mères** Who would argue that the Lyonnais has more first-class chefs than any other region in France? This priceless legacy was conceived over 200 years ago by a series of talented, skilled women: La Mère Guy started it all; La Mère Fillioux was the most famous. During this century others have continued the traditions: La Mère Blanc (Vonnas); La Mère Brazier (30 years ago one of France's few three-star chefs); La Mère Bourgeois (Priay); and La Mère Barattéro (Lamastre).

**Fernand Point** (1899–1956) He was the father of *nouvelle cuisine* and was the first to see, over 50 years ago, that eating habits were changing. He built his menus each day around his purchases at the market; he began to move towards lightness and simplicity. Another contribution to the new ways was his training of Bocuse, Vergé, the Troisgros brothers and others.

**Alexandre Dumaine** A simple man who won for himself a world-wide reputation. He retired in 1963 after working 50 years in kitchens; 30 of them at his Hôtel de la Côte-d'Or in Saulieu (Burgundy). A great chef who used local produce: trout from the Cure; hams from the Morvan; local cheeses; and the best Burgundian wines. He, too, trained many famous chefs of today.

**Paul Bocuse** He is regarded by admirers as the modern-day 'Emperor of chefs' and without any doubt is the best-known *cuisinier* in the world. Won his first Michelin star in 1961 – his third in 1965; a record. Said to have been the greatest advocate of *nouvelle cuisine*, though that hardly applies today. The family auberge, near Lyon, started life in 1765 – Paul Bocuse represents the seventh generation to carry on the tradition.

**Michel Guérard** Widely seen as the greatest innovator of all the new masters. The inventor of *cuisine minceur* (see *Nouvelle Cuisine*), his rejuvenation, as a chef and as a man, came in the mid-1970s: he married Christine Barthélémy and moved to her family's thermal resort hotel at Eugénie-les-Bains. No other chef works in such an inspiring spot; France's best hotel.

**Frédy Girardet** Frédy Girardet towers head and shoulders above the other modern greats. A brilliant Swiss chef, a talented restaurateur (which cannot be said of all chefs), an inspiring leader and a loyal family man; he stays at home in his kitchens and, despite not having the guarantee to fame and fortune that a three-star Michelin rating brings, he is considered by other chefs, critics and sceptics to be the world's greatest 'French' chef.

## *Cheeses* Goat's milk

See the cheeses listed in the neighbouring regions: Côte d'Azur; Hautes-Alpes; and Languedoc-Roussillon

**Picodon de Valréas** soft, nutty-tasting, small disk

**Ewe's milk**

**Brousse du Rove** a creamy, mild-flavoured cheese. At its best in the winter. **Palette** is an ideal wine to drink with it

**Cachat** also known as **Tomme du Mont Ventoux**. A summer season; very soft, sweet and creamy flavour. Drink **Côtes du Ventoux** wines with it

## *Regional Specialities*

See the specialities listed in the Côte d'Azur (pages 32 and 33)

## *Côtes du Rhône Wines* *best years* 78 79 80 81 82 83 85 86

At the northern end of the Rhône Valley, near Vienne, is the **Côte Rôtie**. Some of the oldest and most distinguished of red wines, fine and heady, come from here. So do two marvellous white wines, **Condrieu** and **Château-Grillet** (see page 49).

Further south, from Tain l'Hermitage (**AC Hermitage**, a wonderful wine and **AC Crozes-Hermitage**, a less-good, junior brother), **Saint Joseph** and **Cornas**, all north of Valence, you will find some super, ruby-red wines, dark and powerful. The best of the Rhône reds are made from the Syrah grape. There are also some good dry whites from the same area: a **Hermitage Blanc** (the best is **Chante-Alouette**), a **Saint Péray** white and a **Saint Péray mousseux**. Some whites take the **Crozes-Hermitage** AC (refer to the map and notes on pages 51 and 52).

South-east of Valence, at **Die**, you'll find the lovely **Clairette e Die mousseux**; Clairette grapes for the *brut* version – mainly luscat for the *demi-sec*. Near Die are the wines of all shades om **Châtillon-en-Diois** (see the map on page 37). To the outh of Valence is the **AC Coteaux du Tricastin** and its dry osés and reds (see the map on page 51).

From the southern end of the Rhône Valley come some of the est wines in the region, particularly at **Châteauneuf-du-Pape** with its own AC), a strong, full-bodied red. **Gigondas** (with its wn AC) and **Vacqueyras** are both red and very similar to hâteauneuf-du-Pape; the **Lirac** red is now considered nportant – keep your eyes open for the very rare white Lirac.

**Tavel** was the pioneer among rosés and nearby Lirac makes nother famous one – both are among the best. The Tavel rosé, ightly orange in colour, is made from the Grenache grape.

A fine wine from the lovely area just west of Mont Ventoux is **luscat de Beaumes de Venise**, a delicious, sweet dessert wine. nother one comes from nearby **Rasteau**; the former is made om the Muscat grape – the latter from the Grenache grape.

Many cheaper wines, mainly reds, come from the fringe areas n both the eastern and western edges of the Rhône Valley: mongst them the **AC Côtes du Ventoux**, the VDQS **Côtes du ubéron**, **Côtes du Vivarais** and the **Coteaux de Pierrevert**. nother small VDQS area is **Coteaux des Baux-de-Provence** – ines of all shades but rarely seen other than locally.

The *generic* AC classifications for the whole Rhône area are **ôtes du Rhône** and **Côtes du Rhône-Villages**. 14 villages qualify for the tougher controls of the latter AC: **Chusclan an** **Laudun** in the *département* of Gard; **Cairanne, Vacqueyras** **Rasteau, Valréas, Visan, Roaix** and **Séguret** in Vaucluse;**St Maurice-sur-Aygues, Rousset, Rochegude, St-Pantaléon-les Vignes** and **Vinsobres** in Drôme. One of these controls require the **Villages** wines to have at least 12.5 per cent alcohol as against the 11 per cent for the former AC. The main grape type fo all these southern reds is the Grenache.

**Château d'Estoublon** is near Les Baux-de-Provence **Château Fonsalette** is one of the best Rhône properties.

## *Provence Wines*

Fresh, fragrant whites and rosés are made at **Palette** (east of Aix – look out for **Château Simone**, a property within this AC area) **Cassis, Bandol, Coteaux d'Aix-en-Provence, Côtes de Provence** and **Bellet**, in the Var Valley (see page 33).

Many good reds appear throughout those areas – **Château Vignelaure**, near Rians, is really good, as are the **Bandol** wines

## *Languedoc Wines*

At the northern end of this vast wine-producing mass of countr (see page 43) are some very interesting areas. One is the genera **Costières du Gard** – mainly reds and rosés are made here between Nîmes and Arles is Bellegarde – it has a soun reputation for its dry, white **Clairette de Bellegarde**. Some o the **Coteaux du Languedoc** and **Muscat** wines may appear on wine lists – see page 43 again. **Château de Jau** is one of the bes Roussillon properties.

**Vins de Pays**

You will come across many really sound wines, of all shades. **Vin de Pays des Sables du Golfe du Lion** (around Aigues-Mortes) is especially good; so is the **Vin de Pays du Vaucluse** (the *département* name). Further east are the Var locals or sometime called **Coteaux Varois** (really good bargains). Two other are classifications are **Les Maures** (near St-Tropez) and **Mon Caume** (Bandol area).

If you see the label **Vin de Pays d'Oc** this will mean the win can have originated in any of these five *départements* – **Ardèche Drôme, Var, Bouches-du-Rhône** or **Vaucluse** (or fou *départements* to the south-west – see page 43). Labels may give just the *département* name or, in the case of **Gard**, it may be identified by one of no less than 11 small area names – **Coteau du Salavès** is just one. **Vin de Pays des Coteaux de Baronnie** (Drôme) borders some of the best Rhône areas.

## *Cheeses* Cow's milk

**Abondance** from the hills and valleys encircling the town of the same name. Best in summer and autumn – small, firm wheel

**Beaufort** at its best in winter, spring and summer. A hard, cooked cheese, equivalent to Gruyère, but with no holes. Try it with **Savoie** wines

**Beaumont** mild, creamy, hard disk. Related to Tamié

**Chambarand** made by monks near Roybon. A mild, creamy-tasting, small disk. Ideal with the light wines of **Savoie**

**Colombière** from the Aravis area; mild-flavoured, flat disk

**Fondu aux Raisins (Fondu au Marc)** big disk of processed cheese and covered in grape pips

**Reblochon** best in summer and autumn. Semi-hard, gold colour with a mild and creamy flavour. Made in flat, small disks. A local term – *reblocher* – means 'to milk the cow for the second time'. Try **Crépy** or **Abymes** wines with it or the red from **Chautagne**

**St-Marcellin** available all the year. Small, mild-flavoured disks

**Ste-Foy (Bleu de)** a blue-veined cheese, made in a flat cylinder. Best in summer and autumn. **Bleu de Tignes** is a related cheese

**Sassenage** a summer and autumn season. A soft, spicy-flavoured, blue-vein cheese, related to Bleu de Gex – see Jura region

**Tamié** made by monks at the monastery of the same name, south of Lake Annecy; a light rind and a pressed, uncooked disk

**Tomme de Savoie** a semi-hard, flat cylinder, with a slight nutty smell. A summer and autumn season. Has many relations – all called Tomme

**Vacherin d'Abondance** mild, soft and the size of a thick pancake. At its best in winter. Ideal with **Crépy** or a **Chautagne** wine

## Goat's milk

**Chevrotin des Aravis** a small, flat cylinder with a summer and autumn season. Mild, with no particular smell

**Persillé des Aravis** blue-veined, sharp-tasting, tall cylinder. Also known as **Persillé de Thônes** and **Persillé du Grand-Bornand**

## *Regional Specialities*

**Féra** a freshwater lake fish
**Fondue** hot melted cheese and wine
**Gratin Dauphinois** a classic potato dish with cream, cheese and garlic
**Gratin Savoyard** another classic potato dish with cheese and butter
**Lavaret** a freshwater lake fish, like salmon
**Longeole** a country sausage
**Lotte** a burbot, not unlike an eel
**Omble chevalier** a char, it looks like a large salmon trout

## *Savoie Wines*

### Whites and Rosés

There are many good whites and rosés. The whites from **Seyssel** are delicate and flinty (**Clos de la Peclette** is the best). Another fine white is **Crépy**, made from the Swiss Chasselas grape type this is an AC wine, from the general area south of Lake Geneva The **AC Vin de Savoie** applies to white wines: of these, **Chignin Apremont** and its close neighbour **Abymes** – Abîmes on the maps – (both on the northern slopes of the glorious Chartreuse Massif) are fresh, light and dry; so is the wine called **AC Roussette de Savoie. Roussette de Fragny**, north-east of Seyssel, is a pleasant, subtle wine, as is **Marestel**. These last three are made from the Altesse grape type.

### Reds

**Montmélian** and the neighbouring **Chignin** – both south of Chambéry – are good reds and are made from the Mondeuse grape. Another red is **Chautagne**, made from the Gamay grape, from the vineyards south of Seyssel. These three share the **AC Vin de Savoie**. Often reds will be listed on menus as **Mondeuse** or **Gamay** – their *varietal* names.

### Sparkling wines

Look out for the **Seyssel mousseux, Vin de Savoie mousseux, Vin de Savoie pétillant, Mousseux de Savoie** and **Pétillant de Savoie**. Other sparklers are the rare **Vin de Savoie Ayze mousseux** and **pétillant** (Ayse on the maps). Remember you are in **Chartreuse** country; don't miss those lovely green and yellow liqueurs. Also see page 85 – Chambéry *vermouths*.

### Vin de Pays

These will be labelled by *département* names: **Haute-Savoie, Savoie** and **Isère**.

## *Cheeses* Cow's milk

**Belle des Champs** from Jurançon; white, mild and an aerated texture
**Bethmale** a hard cylinder from the valleys south of St-Gaudens
**Fromage des Pyrénées** a mild, semi-hard, large disk with a hard rind

### Goat's milk

**Cabécous** small, flat cheese. Mild, nutty flavour. At its best in winter

### Ewe's milk

**Esbareich** in the form of a big, flat loaf. A summer and autumn season; ideal with **Madiran**. Related cheeses: **Laruns**, **Amou** and **Ardi-Gasna**
**Iraty** a strong-flavoured, pressed loaf. Contains some cow's milk

## *Regional Specialities*

**Besugo** *daurade* – sea-bream
**Chorizos** spicy sausages
**Confit de canard (d'oie)** preserved duck meat (goose)
**Cousinette (Cousinat)** vegetable soup
**Echassier** a wading bird of the Landes
**Garbure (Garbue)** vegetable soup with cabbage and ham bone
**Gâteau Basque** a shallow, custard pastry – often with fruit fillings
**Grattons (Graisserons)** a *mélange* of small pieces of rendered down pork fat (duck and goose), served as an appetiser – very filling
**Hachua** beef stew
**Jambon de Bayonne** raw ham, cured in salt. Served as paper-thin slices
**Lamproie** eel-like fish, with leeks, onions and red Bordeaux wine sauce
**Lou-kenkas** small, spicy sausages
**Loubine (Louvine)** grey mullet (like a sea-bass)
**Magret (de canard)** breast (of duck)
**Ortolan** a small bird (wheatear) of the Landes
**Ouillat (Ouliat)** Pyrénées soup; onions, tomatoes, goose fat, garlic
**Palombes (Salmis de)** wild doves and wood pigeons from the Landes and Béarn, sautéed in red wine, ham and mushrooms
**Pastiza** see *Gâteau Basque*
**Ramereaux** ring doves
**Salda** a thick cabbage and bean soup
**Tourin (Tourain)** see *Ouillat*. *Touron* – see page 42
**Ttoro (Ttorro)** a Basque fish stew

*Southwest Wines*

In the countryside near **Jurançon** (south-west of Pau), you will find both sweet and dry (*sec*) whites; other whites (of both tastes) to look out for are the strangely-named **Pacherenc du Vic-Bilh** and **Tursan**. From **Madiran** come some excellent reds, which I strongly recommend: **Tursan** (VDQS) also produces some reds. Tursan wines come from the area to the south and west of Eugénie-les-Bains; Vic-Bilh and Madiran wines are made in the country to the east of Eugénie, in the hills before reaching the Adour. North of Condom are the **Côtes de Buzet** – mainly reds, and some whites, are made there. North-west of Plaisance is the newly-promoted VDQS **Côtes de St-Mont** – its reds are good.

Further south try **Irouléguy** wines: red, white and rosé. From the Orthez area come **Béarn** wines, again of all shades. **Armagnac**, France's oldest brandy, is one marvel of the region; many of the restaurants lie in the heart of Armagnac country. The Basques make a liqueur called **Izarra**, meaning *star*; there are two varieties, yellow and green. Enjoy a **Floc** (Armagnac and grape juice) – the Gascon *apéritif*.

**Vins de Pays**

In the Southwest these will be classified by the names of *départements*: **Landes**, **Gers** or **Pyrénées-Atlantiques**. Alternatively, in the Gers area you will see **Vin de Pays des Côtes du Condomois** (from the hills surrounding Condom); **Côtes de Montestruc** and **Côtes de Gascogne** (red and rosé).

*Bordeaux Wines*

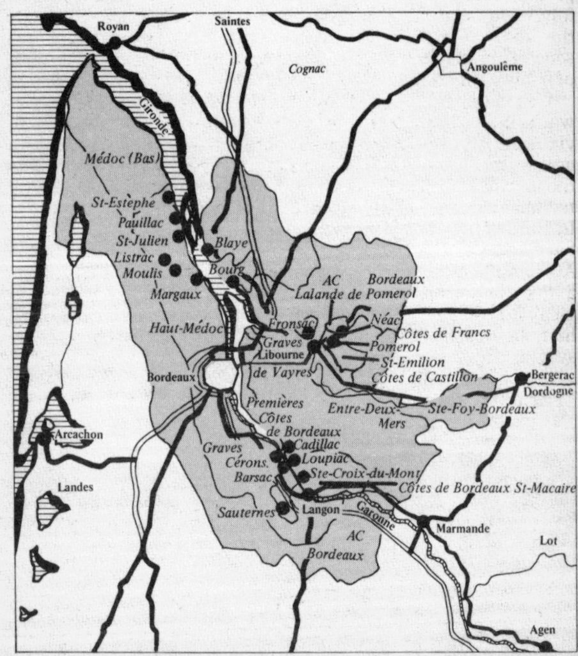

These are outside the geographical limits of the Southwest region but I am including them here for all those travellers in France who love the superb harvests from the vineyards surrounding Bordeaux. This is another area where some of the local wines are beyond the means of most of us. A classic red Bordeaux (called *claret* in the U.K.) is dryer than a Burgundy, less heavy in alcohol, and is really only drinkable when accompanied by food. It has a longer life than a Burgundy red wine.

There are five great wine areas, the first four listed producing reds:

**Médoc**, the largest area and divided into Bas-Médoc and Haut-Médoc. In **Haut-Médoc** is the very famous village of **Pauillac**, from where three of the five great red châteaux wines come.

**Graves** (which means gravelly soil), the second largest area. Whites also are made here.

**St-Emilion** and **Pomerol**, much smaller areas and both on the banks of the Dordogne.

**Sauternes** is the fifth area, famous for its white wines.

Some of the best-known wines in the world come from the vineyards of Bordeaux: amongst the reds are **Château Lafite**, **Château Latour** and **Château Mouton-Rothschild** (all three in the village of Pauillac); **Château Margaux**, also in the Haut-Médoc; and **Château Haut-Brion** from Graves. These five reds are at the top of the pyramid, the *Premiers Crus* (first growths). It is a white from Sauternes, **Château d'Yquem**, that has a special rank above even those five, *Premier Grand Cru*. Dozens and dozens of other châteaux follow, split into various levels of prestige, rather than excellence of quality – see the lists that follow on page 71. Thankfully, there are many clarets towards the bottom of the pyramid (see *Crus Bourgeois*) which are sensibly priced; the Bordeaux area producing a high proportion of quality wine for all of us, whatever the size of our pockets.

We need to understand how the Appellation Contrôlée system works in Bordeaux. Think of a pyramid: the wines from a specific vineyard, perhaps just as big as a football field, sit at the top and are the most expensive. The bottom of the pyramid represents those wines from any part of the whole region, the ones that do not have a pedigree in the form of their own individual AC status. In Bordeaux, unlike Burgundy, an individual château does not have its own AC; it will share the *commune*, or even the region's, AC classification. Do not imagine the term *château* always means a fine, imposing building; more often than not it refers to vineyards making up an estate, the only building perhaps being a humble shed, half-buried, where the wine is stored. How does the system work?

1. A bottle label with **AC Bordeaux** or **AC Bordeaux-Supérieur** (this means higher alcohol strength, not superior quality) is wine that has come from anywhere in the entire region; it will certainly be from the fringe areas and it will be the cheapest wine.
2. A label with **AC Médoc** indicates it comes from that general area to the north-west of Bordeaux, on the west bank of the Gironde. This will be both dearer and better wine. It is likely it will be from the Bas-Médoc, considered inferior to Haut-Médoc.
3. A label with **AC Haut-Médoc** will signify it was produced in that specific part of the Médoc considered superior for vineyard quality. These wines will be further up the quality and price scale.

All three examples are *generic* wines, those carrying the name of a geographical area, though many of them, even some in example 1, may still carry a château name.

4 A label with **AC Pauillac** means the wine was made in that *commune* within the Haut-Médoc. It will be getting expensive and will be an excellent claret. Most labels will be carrying a château name as well, from the humble to a few like **AC Pauillac Château Lafite**; this label would indicate that not only have you a specific vineyard in Pauillac but also one of the top five reds in Bordeaux.

**Reds** *best years* **71 75 76 78 79 81 82 83 85 86**

There are dozens of good clarets available at relatively modest cost. Clearly the first three examples I have mentioned qualify and some from the fourth example. So do wines from other Haut-Médoc *communes*: from north to south, **Saint Estèphe**, **Saint Julien**, **Listrac**, **Moulis** and **Margaux**; all have their own AC.

Wines from the other great red areas qualify: **Graves**, **Pomerol** (**Château Pétrus** is thought by many to be amongst the best of all Bordeaux wines) and **Saint Emilion**. Saint Emilion has three extra AC levels: its best châteaux are classified as **Saint Emilion Premier Grand Cru Classé** and some 70 others as **Saint Emilion Grand Cru Classé**. A lower rating is **Saint Emilion Grand Cru**. Saint Emilion is bordered by five smaller *communes*, all having their own AC with the addition of the word **Saint Emilion**: **Lussac**, **Montagne**, **Parsac**, **Puissegiun** and **Saint Georges**. Other reds from lesser-known areas are (from north to south): **Premières Côtes de Blaye**, **Bourg**, **Cotes de Bourg** (considered better), **Côtes de Fronsac**, **Fronsac**, **Côtes Canon Fronsac**, **Lalande de Pomerol**, **Néac**, **Bordeaux Côtes de Francs** and **Bordeaux (Supérieur) Côtes de Castillon**, these last two being just east of Saint Emilion.

Other areas are the **Premières Côtes de Bordeaux**, on the east bank of the Garonne; **Graves de Vayres**; **Bordeaux Haut Benauge** (part of the Entre-Deux-Mers territory). **AC Bordeaux** or **AC Bordeaux Supérieur** are the most common reds.

**Rosés**

Rarely seen are the **Bordeaux Clairet** and **Bordeaux Supérieur Clairet** – wines with a shorter fermentation period and thus dark rosé in colour; equally rare are the **AC Bordeaux Rosé** and the **AC Bordeaux Supérieur Rosé**.

**Whites** *best years* **70 71 75 78 81 82 83 85 86**

The white wines of Bordeaux have gone through a significant transition during recent years. Because of both the increasing demand for dry wines and the crippling costs of producing sweet, dessert wines, growers have responded by making crisp, light whites – lovely wines and cheap, too. Dry white wines will normally be in green bottles – sweet ones in clear glass.

Of the various whites made from the Sauvignon Blanc grape, look out for the crisp drys of **Entre-Deux-Mers**, **Entre-Deux-Mers-Haut Benauge** and **Graves de Vayres**. A white **AC Bordeaux** will be a dry alternative as will **Blaye**, **Côtes de Blaye**, **Côtes de Bourg** and **Graves**. From **Côtes de Bordeaux Saint Macaire**, north of Langon, **Premières Côtes de Bordeaux** and **Ste-Foy-Bordeaux** come both dry and sweet wines.

For those of you with a sweet tooth the golden **Sauternes**, **Barsac**, **Cérons**, **Loupiac**, **Sainte Croix-du-Mont** and **Cadillac** will be the answer (the Sémillon grape is the most common – ideal with its high sugar content). **AC Bordeaux Supérieur** and **Graves Supérieur** will be medium-sweet, golden white alternatives. An AC is also given to a **Bordeaux mousseux**.

*Great Growths (Grands Crus) of the Médoc – 1855 list*

| Château | AC taken |
|---|---|
| **First Growths** *(Premiers Crus)* | |
| Lafite | *Pauillac* |
| Latour | *Pauillac* |
| Margaux | *Margaux* |
| Haut-Brion (not in Médoc) | *Graves* |
| Mouton-Rothschild (1973) | *Pauillac* |
| **Second Growths** *(Seconds Crus)* | |
| Brane-Cantenac | *Margaux* |
| Cos d'Estournel | *St-Estèphe* |
| Ducru-Beaucaillou | *St-Julien* |
| Durfort-Vivens | *Margaux* |
| Gruaud-Larose | *St-Julien* |
| Lascombes | *Margaux* |
| Léoville-Barton | *St-Julien* |
| Léoville-Las-Cases | *St-Julien* |
| Léoville-Poyferré | *St-Julien* |
| Montrose | *St-Estèphe* |
| Pichon-Longueville and Pichon-Longueville-Lalande | *Pauillac* |
| Rauzan-Gassies | *Margaux* |
| Rausan-Ségla | *Margaux* |
| **Third Growths** *(Troisièmes Crus)* | |
| Boyd-Cantenac | *Margaux* |
| Calon-Ségur | *St-Estèphe* |
| Cantenac-Brown | *Margaux* |
| Desmirail | *Margaux* |
| Ferrière | *Margaux* |
| Giscours | *Margaux* |
| d'Issan | *Margaux* |
| Kirwan | *Margaux* |
| Lagrange | *St-Julien* |
| Langoa | *St-Julien* |
| La Lagune | *Haut-Médoc* |
| Malescot-St-Exupéry | *Margaux* |

| Château | AC taken |
|---|---|
| **Third Growths** *(Troisièmes Crus)* | |
| Marquis d'Alesme-Becker | *Margaux* |
| Palmer | *Margaux* |
| **Fourth Growths** *(Quatrièmes Crus)* | |
| Beychevelle | *St-Julien* |
| Branaire-Ducru | *St-Julien* |
| Duhart-Milon | *Pauillac* |
| Lafon-Rochet | *St-Estèphe* |
| La Tour-Carnet | *Haut-Médoc* |
| Marquis-de-Terme | *Margaux* |
| Pouget | *Margaux* |
| Prieuré-Lichine | *Margaux* |
| St-Pierre-Bontemps | *St-Julien* |
| St-Pierre-Sevaistre | *St-Julien* |
| Talbot | *St-Julien* |
| **Fifth Growths** *(Cinquièmes Crus)* | |
| Batailley | *Pauillac* |
| Belgrave | *Haut-Médoc* |
| Camensac | *Haut-Médoc* |
| Cantemerle | *Haut-Médoc* |
| Clerc-Milon | *Pauillac* |
| Cos Labory | *St-Estèphe* |
| Croizet-Bages | *Pauillac* |
| Dauzac | *Margaux* |
| du Tertre | *Margaux* |
| Grand-Puy-Ducasse | *Pauillac* |
| Grand-Puy-Lacoste | *Pauillac* |
| Haut-Bages-Libéral | *Pauillac* |
| Haut-Batailley | *Pauillac* |
| Lynch-Bages | *Pauillac* |
| Lynch-Moussas | *Pauillac* |
| Mouton-Baronne-Philippe | *Pauillac* |
| Pédesclaux | *Pauillac* |
| Pontel-Canet | *Pauillac* |

Then follow about 160 *Crus Bourgeois* properties – making quality wines at lower prices than the classified growths listed above. Until recently there were two additional classifications – *Cru Grand Bourgeois* and *Cru Bourgeois Exceptionnel*: the EEC objected to these terms and now all of them are called *Crus Bourgeois*.

*First Great Growths (Premiers Grands Crus) of St-Emilion*

12 châteaux share this 1955 classification:

Ausone, Cheval-Blanc, Beauséjour-Duffau-Lagarrosse, Beauséjour-Becot, Bel-Air, Canon, Figeac, Clos Fourtet, La Gaffelière, La Magdelaine, Pavie, Trottevieille.

*Classified Growths of the Graves: the best châteaux*

**Red wines**: Bouscaut, Haut-Bailly, Carbonnieux, Domaine de Chevalier, Fieuzal, Olivier, Malartic-Lagravière, La Tour-Martillac, Smith-Haut-Lafitte, Haut-Brion (see *Médoc* list) – and its excellent white wine as well, La Mission-Haut-Brion, Pape Clément, Latour-Haut-Brion.

**White wines**: Bouscaut, Carbonnieux, Domaine de Chevalier, Olivier, Malartic-Lagravière, La Tour-Martillac, Laville-Haut-Brion, Couhins.

*1855 Classification of Sauternes and Barsac châteaux*

*Premier Grand Cru* – the only one in Bordeaux: d'Yquem.

*Premiers Crus*: Climens, Coutet, de Rayne-Vigneau, de Suduiraut, Guiraud, Haut-Peyraguey, Lafaurie-Peyraguey, La Tour-Blanche, Rabaud-Promis, Rieussec, Sigalas-Rebaud.

*Seconds Crus*: Broustet, Caillou, d'Arche, de Malle, de Myrat, Doisy-Daëne, Doisy-Védrines, Filhot, Lamothe, Nairac, Romer, Suau.

## CORSICA

23

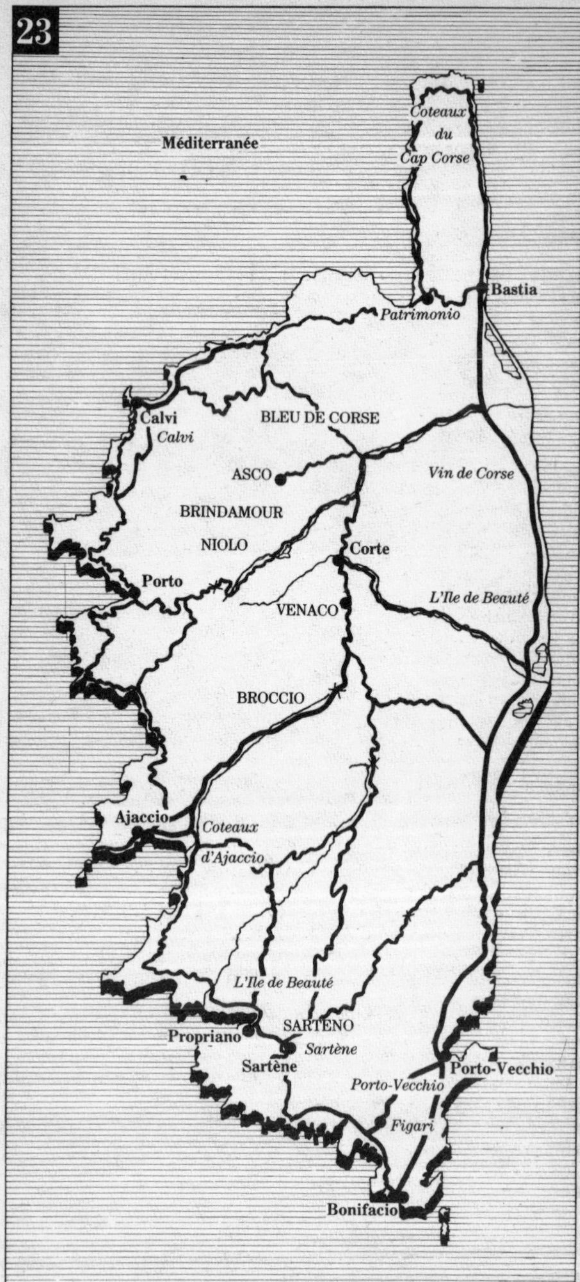

Méditerranée
Coteaux du Cap Corse
Bastia
Patrimonio
Calvi
Calvi
BLEU DE CORSE
ASCO
Vin de Corse
BRINDAMOUR
NIOLO
Corte
Porto
L'Ile de Beauté
VENACO
BROCCIO
Ajaccio
Coteaux d'Ajaccio
L'Ile de Beauté
SARTENO
Propriano
Sartène
Sartène
Porto-Vecchio
Porto-Vecchio
Figari
Bonifacio

*Cheeses* **Goat's milk**

**Brindamour** also known as **Fleur du Maquis**. A small square, covered with the herbs rosemary and savory. Best season is summer. Some versions of neighbouring **Asco** are similar

**Niolo** similar shape to Brindamour but with no herb covering. Very sharp taste — can also be made with ewe's milk. **Asco** is a related cheese

**Sarteno** an uncooked, pressed and flattened ball with a sharp taste. Often made from ewe's milk

**Venaco** can also be made from ewe's milk. Same shape as Niolo. Strong, sharp smell and taste. Cured in caves

**Ewe's milk**

**Broccio (Brocciu)** a fresh cheese made by heating and beating the milk. Packed in small baskets. Often served with cream and sugar. Used in many Corsican desserts

**Corse (Bleu de)** a blue cheese made in tall cylinders — cured in caves at Roquefort (see page 51) and with a similar taste to that world-famous sharp tasting cheese

*Regional Specialities*

**Aziminu** the Corsican *bouillabaisse*. Large *rascasse* (called *capone* or *capoum*), red peppers and pimentos are among the local ingredients

**Canistrelli** an almond cake flavoured with *anis*

**Cédrat** a sour lemon-like fruit used in sweets and liqueurs

**Falculelle (Falculella)** a cheesecake using Broccio cheese

**Fiadone** an orange-flavoured flan made with Broccio cheese

**Frittelle** chestnut flour fritters

**Panizze** a fried cake — made from chestnut flour (or cornmeal)

**Piverunata (Pebronata)** a stew of kid (young goat), or beef, or chicken — in a sauce of red peppers, garlic and tomatoes

**Pulenta (Polenta)** in Corsica this is usually made from chestnut flour — similar in appearance to the Italian boiled commercial version

**Stufatu** the Italian influence is strong in Corsican cooking — particularly pasta. This dish is macaroni with mushrooms and onions

**Torta castagina** a tart covered with crushed almonds, *pignons, raisins secs* and rum

**Ziminu** a pimento and red pepper sauce for fish

*Wines*

There are eight *appellation contrôlée* names for the island's wines. The most basic wine is **Vin de Corse**. This Vin de Corse prefix forms part of the other seven classifications — followed by local area names: **Coteaux du Cap Corse** and **Patrimonio** (both near Bastia); **Coteaux d'Agaccio, Sartène, Figari, Porto-Vecchio** (all in the south); and **Calvi**. You'll find dry whites, fruity rosés (the best comes from grapes macerated for one night) and strong reds.

Look out for the sweet Muscat and Malvoisie (Malmsey) grape type wines. Cap Corse also gives its name to a well-known *apéritif*.

Enjoy the Corsican versions of *eaux-de-vie* — colourless liqueurs distilled from fermented fruit juices: *arbouse* — fruit of the strawberry tree is a Corsican rarity. Relish, too, *cédratine* — a rich, sweet liqueur made from *cédrat*, a sour lemon-like fruit.

**Vins de Pays**

These are called **L'Ile de Beauté**.

 *(also see foot of page 84)*

**Abatis (Abattis)** poultry giblets
**Abats** offal
**Ablette** freshwater fish
**Abricots** apricots
**Acarne** sea-bream
**Acidulé(e)** acid
**Affiné(e)** refined
**Africaine (à l')** African style: with aubergines, tomatoes, *cèpes*
**Agneau** lamb
**Agneau de pré-salé** lamb fed on salt marshes
**Agnelet** young lamb
**Agnès Sorel** thin strips of mushroom, chicken and tongue
**Aiglefin** haddock
**Aigre-doux** sweet-sour
**Aiguillettes** thin slices
**Ail** garlic
**Aile** wing
**Aileron** winglet
**Aïoli** mayonnaise, garlic, olive oil
**Airelles** cranberries
**Albert** white cream sauce, mustard, vinegar
**Albuféra** *béchamel* sauce, sweet peppers
**Alénois** watercress-flavoured
**Algues** seaweed
**Aligot** purée of potatoes, *Tomme* cheese, cream, garlic, butter
**Allemande** *velouté* sauce with egg yolks
**Allemande (à l')** German style: with sauerkraut and sausages
**Allumettes** puff pastry strips
**Alose** shad
**Alouette** lark
**Alouette de mer** sandpiper
**Aloyau** sirloin of beef
**Alsacienne (à l')** Alsace style: with sauerkraut, sausage and sometimes *foie gras*
**Amandes** almonds
**Amandine** almond-flavoured
**Amer** bitter
**Américaine (à l') Armoricaine (à la)** sauce with dry white wine, cognac, tomatoes, shallots
**Amourettes** ox or calf marrow
**Amusettes** appetisers
**Ananas** pineapple
**Anchoïade** anchovy crusts
**Anchois** anchovy
**Ancienne (à l')** in the 'old style'
**Andalouse (à l')** Andalusian style: tomatoes, sweet red peppers, rice
**Andouille** cold smoked sausage
**Andouillette** chitterling (tripe) sausage
**Aneth** dill
**Ange** angel
**Angevine (à l')** Anjou style: wi[th] dry white wine, cream, mus[h]rooms, onions
**Anglaise (à l')** plain boiled
**Anguilles** eels
**Anis** aniseed
**Arachides** peanuts
**Araignée de mer** spider crab
**Ardennaise (à l')** Ardenne sty[le] with juniper berries
**Argenteuil** asparagus flavour[ed] (usually soup)
**Arlésienne** stuffed tomatoes *à [la] provençale*, eggplant, rice
**Armoricaine** see *Américaine*
**Aromates** aromatic – either spi[cy] or fragrant
**Artichaut** artichoke
**Asperges** asparagus
**Assiette (de)** plate (of)
**Aubergine** aubergine, eggplant
**Aulx** (plural of *ail*) garlic
**Aumonière** pancake
**Aurore (à l')** pink sauce, toma[to] flavoured
**Auvergnate (à l')** Auvergne styl[e] with cabbage, sausage and bacon
**Avelines** hazelnuts
**Avocat** avocado pear
**Baba au rhum** sponge with ru[m] syrup
**Baguette** long bread loaf
**Baies** berries
**Baigné** bathed or lying in
**Ballotine** boned and stuffe[d] poultry or meat in a roll
**Banane** banana
**Bar** sea-bass
**Barbarie** Barbary duck
**Barbeau** barbel
**Barbue** brill
**Barigoule (à la)** brown sauce wi[th] artichokes and mushrooms
**Baron de lapereau** baron of youn[g] rabbit
**Barquette** boat-shaped pastry
**Basilic** basil
**Basquaise (à la)** Basque styl[e] Bayonne ham, rice and peppers
**Bâtarde** butter sauce, egg yolks
**Baudroie** monkfish, anglerfish
**Bavaroise** bavarois mould, usuall[y] of custard, flavoured with fruit [or] chocolate. Can describe othe[r] dishes – particularly shellfish
**Bavette** skirt of beef
**Béarnaise** thick sauce with eg[g] yolks, shallots, butter, white win[e]

and tarragon vinegar
**Béatilles (Malin de)** sweetbreads, livers, kidneys, cocks' combs
**Beaugency** *Béarnaise* sauce, artichokes, tomatoes, marrow
**Bécasse** woodcock
**Bécassine** snipe
**Béchamel** creamy white sauce
**Beignets** fritters
**Belons** flat-shelled oysters
**Bercy** sauce with white wine and shallots
**Berrichone** *Bordelaise* sauce
**Betterave** beetroot
**Beuchelle à la Tourangelle** kidneys, sweetbreads, morels, truffles, cream
**Beurre** butter
**Beurre blanc** sauce with butter, shallots, wine vinegar and sometimes dry white wine
**Beurre noir** sauce with browned butter, vinegar, parsley
**Bifteck** steak
**Bigarade (à la)** orange sauce
**Bigarreau** type of cherry
**Bigorneaux** winkles
**Billy By** mussel soup
**Biscuit à la cuiller** sponge finger
**Bisque** shellfish soup
**Blanc (de volaille)** white breast (of chicken): can describe white fish fillet or white vegetables
**Blanchailles** whitebait
**Blanquette** white stew
**Blettes** Swiss chard
**Blinis** small, thick pancakes
**Bœuf à la mode** beef braised in red wine
**Bœuf Stroganoff** beef, sour cream, onions, mushrooms
**Bombe** ice cream
**Bonne femme (à la)** white wine sauce, shallots, mushrooms
**Bonne femme (à la)** potato, leek, carrot soup
**Bordelais(e) (à la)** Bordeaux style: brown sauce with shallots, red wine and beef bone marrow
**Bouchée** mouthful size (either a tart or *vol-au-vent*)
**Boudin** sausage-shaped pudding
**Boudin blanc** white coloured – pork and sometimes chicken
**Boudin noir** black pudding
**Bouillabaisse** Mediterranean fish stew and soup – see Côte d'Azur
**Bouillon** broth, light consommé
**Boulangère** sauce of onions, potatoes
**Boulette** small ball of fish or meat
**Bouquet** prawn
**Bourdaloue** hot poached fruit
**Bourdelot** whole apple pastry
**Bourgeoise (à la)** sauce of carrots, onions, diced bacon
**Bourguignonne (à la)** Burgundy style: red wine, onions, bacon, mushrooms
**Bourride** creamy fish soup with *aïoli*
**Braisé** braised
**Brandade de morue** salt cod
**Bréjaude** cabbage and bacon soup
**Brème** bream
**Brési** thin slices dried beef
**Bretonne** sauce with celery, leeks, beans, mushrooms
**Brioche** sweet yeast bread roll
**Broche (à la)** spit roasted
**Brochet** pike
**Brochette (de)** meat or fish on a skewer
**Brouet** broth
**Brouillade** stewed in oil
**Brouillés** scrambled
**Broutard** young goat
**Brugnon** nectarine
**Brûlé** toasted
**Brunoise** diced vegetables
**Bruxelloise** sauce with asparagus, butter, eggs
**Bugnes** sweet pastry fritters
**Cabillaud** cod
**Caen (à la mode de)** cooked in Calvados and white wine
**Café** coffee
**Cagouilles** snails
**Caille (Caillette)** quail
**Calmars** inkfish, squid
**Campagne** country style
**Canapé** a base, usually bread
**Canard** duck
**Canard à la presse (Rouennaise)** duck breast cooked in blood of carcass, red wine and brandy
**Canard sauvage** wild duck
**Caneton (canette)** duckling
**Cannelle** cinnamon
**Capilotade** small bits or pieces
**Capoum** scorpion fish
**Caprice** *whim* (desserts)
**Capucine** nasturtium
**Carbonnade** braised beef in beer, onions and bacon
**Cardinal** *béchamel* sauce, lobster, cream, red peppers
**Cardons** large celery-like vegetable
**Caroline** chicken consommé

**Carpe** carp
**Carré d'agneau** lamb chops from best end of neck
**Carré de porc** pork cutlets from best end of neck
**Carré de veau** veal chops from best end of neck
**Carrelet** flounder, plaice
**Carvi** caraway seeds
**Casse-croûte** snack
**Cassis** blackcurrants
**Cassolette** small pan
**Cassoulet** casserole of beans, pork or goose or duck
**Céleri** celery
**Céleri-rave** celeriac
**Cèpes** fine, delicate mushrooms
**Cerfeuil** chervil
**Cerises (noires)** cherries (black)
**Cerneaux** walnuts
**Cervelas** pork garlic sausage
**Cervelle** brains
**Champignons (des bois)** mushrooms (from the woods)
**Chanterelles** apricot-coloured mushrooms
**Chantilly** whipped cream, sugar
**Chapon** capon
**Chapon de mer** *rascasse* or scorpion fish
**Charcuterie** cold cut meats
**Charcutière** sauce with onions, white wine, gherkins
**Charlotte** sweet of sponge fingers, cream, etc.
**Charolais (Charollais)** beef
**Chartreuse** a mould form
**Chasse** hunting (season)
**Chasseur** sauce with white wine, mushrooms, shallots
**Châtaignes** chestnuts
**Châteaubriand** thick fillet steak
**Châtelaine** garnish with artichoke hearts, tomatoes, potatoes
**Chaud(e)** hot
**Chaudrée** fish stew
**Chausson** pastry turnover with various fillings
**Chemise (en)** pastry covering
**Chevreuil** roe-deer
**Chicon** chicory
**Chicorée** curly endive
**Chiffonnade** thinly-cut
**Chinoise (à la)** Chinese style: with bean sprouts and soy sauce
**Chiperones** see *calmars*
**Choisy** braised lettuce, sautéed potatoes
**Choron** *Béarnaise* sauce with tomato

**Chou (vert)** cabbage
**Choucroute** sauerkraut, peppercorns, boiled ham, potatoes, Strasbourg sausages
**Chou-fleur** cauliflower
**Chou-pommé** white-heart cabbage
**Chou rouge** red cabbage
**Choux (au fromage)** puffs (cheese)
**Choux de Bruxelles** Brussels sprouts
**Ciboules** spring onions
**Ciboulettes** chives
**Cidre** cider
**Citron** lemon
**Citron vert** lime
**Civet** stew
**Civet de lièvre** jugged hare
**Clafoutis** tart (usually cherries)
**Claires** oysters (see page 60)
**Clamart** with petits pois
**Clouté (de)** studded with
**Cochon** pig
**Cochonnailles** pork products
**Cocotte (en)** cooking pot
**Cœur (de)** heart (of)
**Coffret (en)** in a *small box*
**Coing** quince
**Colbert (à la)** fish, dipped in milk egg and breadcrumbs
**Colin** hake
**Colvert** wild duck
**Compote** stewed or preserved fruit
**Concassée** coarsely chopped
**Concombres** cucumbers
**Condé** creamed rice and fruit
**Confit(e)** preserved or candied
**Confiture** jam
**Confiture d'oranges** marmalade
**Congre** conger eel
**Consommé** clear soup
**Contrefilet** sirloin, usually tied for roasting
**Copeaux** literally *shavings*
**Coq (au vin)** chicken in red wine sauce (or name of wine)
**Coque (à la)** soft-boiled – or served in shell
**Coquelet** young cockerel
**Coques** cockles
**Coquillages** shellfish
**Coquilles St-Jacques** scallops
**Corail (de)** coral (of)
**Coriandre** coriander
**Cornichons** gherkins
**Côte d'agneau** lamb chop
**Côte de bœuf** side of beef
**Côte de veau** veal chop

**Côtelette** chop

**Cou (d'oie)** neck (of goose)

**Coulibiac** hot salmon *tourte*

**Coulis (de)** thick sauce (of)

**Coupe** ice cream dessert

**Courge** pumpkin

**Courgettes** baby marrows

**Couronne** circle or ring

**Court-bouillon** aromatic poaching liquid

**Crabe** crab

**Crapaudine (à la)** grilled game bird with backbone removed

**Crécy** with carrots and rice

**Crème** cream

**Crème (à la)** served with cream or cooked in cream sauce

**Crème à l'anglaise** light custard sauce

**Crème brûlée** same, less sugar and cream and with praline

**Crème pâtissière** custard filling

**Crème plombières** custard filling: egg whites, fresh fruit flavouring

**Crêpe** thin pancake

**Crêpes Suzette** sweet pancakes with orange liqueur sauce

**Crépinette (de)** wrapping (of)

**Cresson** watercress

**Cressonière** purée of potatoes, watercress

**Crêtes** cockscombs

**Creuse** long, thick-shelled oyster

**Crevettes grises** shrimps

**Crevettes roses** prawns

**Cromesquis** croquettes

**Croque Monsieur** toasted cheese or ham sandwich

**Croquette** see *boulette*

**Croustade** small pastry mould with various fillings

**Croûte (en)** pastry crust (in a)

**Croûtons** bread (toast or fried)

**Cru** raw

**Crudités** raw vegetables

**Crustacés** shellfish

**Cuillère** soft (cut with spoon)

**Cuisses (de)** legs (of)

**Cuissot (de)** haunch (of)

**Cuit** cooked

**Cul** haunch or rear

**Culotte** rump (usually steak)

**Cultivateur** soup of chopped vegetables

**Dariole** basket-shaped pastry

**Darne** slice or steak

**Dattes** dates

**Daube** stew (various types)

**Daurade** sea-bream

**Dégustation** tasting

**Délice** delight

**Demi-glace** basic brown sauce

**Demi-sel** lightly salted

**Diable** seasoned with mustard

**Diane (à la)** peppered cream sauce

**Dieppoise (à la)** Dieppe style: white wine, cream, mussels, shrimps

**Dijonnaise (à la)** with mustard sauce

**Dijonnaise (à la belle)** blackcurrant sauce

**Dinde** young hen turkey

**Dindon** turkey

**Dindonneau** young turkey

**Dodine (de canard)** cold stuffed duck

**Dorade** dorado

**Doria** with cucumbers

**Douceurs** desserts

**Doux (douce)** sweet

**Du Barry** cauliflower soup

**Duxelles** chopped mushrooms, shallots and cream

**Echalotes** shallots

**Echine** spare ribs

**Echiquier** *checkered* fashion

**Ecrevisses** freshwater crayfish

**Ecuelle** bowl or basin

**Effiloché(e)** frayed, thinly sliced

**Emincé** thinly sliced

**Encornets** cuttlefish

**Endive** chicory

**Entrecôte** entrecôte, rib steak

**Entremets** sweets

**Epaule** shoulder

**Eperlan** smelt

**Epices** spices

**Epinards** spinach

**Epis de maïs** sweetcorn

**Escabèche** fish (or poultry) marinated in *court-bouillon* – cold

**Escalope** thinly cut (meat or fish)

**Escargots** snails

**Espadon** swordfish

**Estouffade** stew with onions, herbs, mushrooms, red or white wine (perhaps garlic)

**Estragon** tarragon flavoured

**Etrilles** crabs

**Etuvé(e)** cooked in little water or in ingredient's own juice

**Exocet** flying fish

**Façon** cooked in a described way

**Faisan(e)** pheasant

**Farci(e)** stuffed

**Farine** flour

**Faux-filet** sirloin steak

**Favorite** garnish *foie gras*, truffles

**Favouilles** spider crabs
**Fenouil** fennel
**Féra** freshwater lake fish
**Ferme (fermier)** farm (farmer)
**Fermière** mixture of onions, carrots, turnips, celery, etc.
**Feuille de vigne** vine leaf
**Feuilleté** light flaky pastry
**Fèves** broad beans
**Ficelle (à la)** tied in a string
**Ficelles** thin loaves of bread
**Figues** figs
**Filet** fillet
**Financière (à la)** Madeira sauce with truffles
**Fines herbes** mixture of parsley, chives, tarragon, etc.
**Flageolets** kidney beans
**Flamande (à la)** Flemish style
**Flambé** flamed
**Flamiche** puff pastry tart
**Flan** tart
**Flétan** halibut
**Fleur** flower
**Fleurons** puff pastry crescents
**Florentine** with spinach
**Foie** liver
**Foie gras** goose liver
**Foies blonds de volaille** chicken liver mousse
**Foin (dans le)** cooked in hay
**Fond** (base) basic stock
**Fondant** see *boulette*: a *bon-bon*
**Fonds d'artichauts** artichoke hearts
**Fondue (de fromage)** melted (cheese with wine)
**Forestière** with bacon and mushrooms
**Four (au)** baked in oven
**Fourré** stuffed
**Frais, fraîche** fresh or cool
**Fraises** strawberries
**Fraises des bois** wild strawberries
**Framboises** raspberries
**Française (à la)** mashed potato filled with mixed vegetables
**Frangipane** almond custard filling
**Frappé** frozen or ice cold
**Friandises** sweets – *petits fours*
**Fricadelles** minced meat balls
**Fricandeau** slice topside veal
**Fricassée** braised in sauce or butter, egg yolks and cream
**Frisé(e)** curly
**Frit** fried
**Frites** chips
**Fritot** fritter
**Frittons** see *grattons*
**Friture** small fried fish
**Frivolles** fritters
**Froid** cold
**Fromage** cheese
**Fromage de tête** brawn
**Fruit de la passion** passion fruit
**Fruits confits** crystallised fruit
**Fruits de mer** seafood
**Fumé** smoked
**Fumet** fish stock
**Galantine** cooked meat, fish o[r] vegetables in jelly – served cold
**Galette** pastry, pancake or cake
**Galimafrée (de)** stew (of)
**Gambas** big prawns
**Garbure (Garbue)** vegetable sou[p]
**Gardons** small roach
**Garni(e)** with vegetables
**Garniture** garnish
**Gâteau** cake
**Gâtinaise (à la)** with honey
**Gaufre** waffle
**Gayettes** faggots
**Gelée** aspic jelly
**Géline** chicken
**Genièvre** juniper
**Génoise** rich sponge cake
**Germiny** sorrel and cream soup
**Gésier** gizzard
**Gibelotte** see *fricassée*
**Gibier** game
**Gigot (de)** leg (of lamb) – ca[n] describe other things
**Gigue (de)** shank (of)
**Gingembre** ginger
**Girofle** clove
**Girolles** apricot-coloured fungi
**Glacé** iced. Crystallised. Glazed
**Glace** ice cream
**Godard** see *financière (à la)*
**Gougère** round-shaped, egg an[d] cheese *chou* pastry
**Goujonnettes (de)** small frie[d] pieces (of)
**Goujons** gudgeon
**Gourmandises** sweetmeats – ca[n] describe *fruits de mer*
**Gousse (de)** pod or husk (of)
**Graine (de capucine)** see[d] (nasturtium)
**Graisse** fat
**Graisserons** duck and goose fa[t] scratchings
**Grand Veneur** sauce with vegetables, wine vinegar, redcurran[t] jelly and cream
**Granité** water ice
**Gratin** browned
**Gratin Dauphinois** potato dish with cream, cheese, garlic
**Gratin Savoyard** potato dish with cheese and butter

**Gratiné** top of sauced dish browned with butter, cheese, etc.
**Grattons** pork scratchings
**Gravettes** oysters
**Grecque (à la)** cooked vegetables served cold
**Grenade** pomegranate
**Grenadin** thick veal escalope
**Grenouilles** frogs
**Grillade** grilled meat
**Grillé(e)** grilled
**Griottes** bitter red cherries
**Grisets** mushrooms
**Grive** thrush
**Grondin** gurnard, red gurnet
**Gros sel** coarse rock or sea salt
**Groseilles** gooseberries
**Groseilles noires** blackcurrants
**Groseilles rouges** redcurrants
**Gruyère** hard, mild cheese
**Gyromitres** fungi
**Habit vert** *dressed* in green
**Hachis** minced or chopped-up
**Hareng** herring
**Hareng fumé** kippered
**Hareng salé** bloater
**Haricot (de)** stew (of)
**Haricots** beans
**Haricots blancs** white beans (dried)
**Haricots rouges** kidney beans
**Haricots verts** green beans or French beans
**Hochepot** thick stew
**Hollandaise** sauce with butter, egg yolk, lemon juice
**Homard** lobster
**Hongroise (à la)** Hungarian style: sauce with tomato, paprika
**Hors d'œuvre** appetisers
**Huile** oil
**Huîtres** oysters (see page 60)
**Hure (de)** head (of). Brawn. Jellied
**Ile flottante** unmoulded soufflé of beaten egg white and sugar
**Imam bayeldi** aubergine with rice, onions and sautéed tomatoes
**Impératrice (à la)** desserts with candied fruits soaked in *kirsch*
**Indienne (à l')** Indian style: with curry powder
**Italienne (à l')** Italian style: artichokes, mushrooms, pasta
**Jambon** ham
**Jambonneau** knuckle of pork
**Jambonnette (de)** boned and stuffed (knuckle of ham or poultry)
**Jardinière** diced fresh vegetables
**Jarret de veau** stew of shin of veal
**Jarretons** cooked pork knuckles
**Jésus de Morteau** – smoked Jura pork sausage
**Joinville** *velouté* sauce with cream, crayfish tails, truffles
**Joue (de)** cheek (of)
**Judru** cured pork sausage
**Julienne** thinly-cut vegetables. See *lingue*
**Jus** juice
**Lait** milk
**Laitance** soft roe
**Laitue** lettuce
**Lamproie** eel-like fish
**Langouste** spiny lobster or crawfish
**Langoustines** Dublin Bay prawns
**Langue** tongue
**Languedocienne (à la)** mushrooms, tomatoes, parsley garnish
**Lapereau** young rabbit
**Lapin** rabbit
**Lapin de garenne** wild rabbit
**Lard** bacon
**Lard de poitrine** fat belly of pork
**Lardons** strips of bacon
**Lavaret** freshwater lake fish
**Lèche** thin slice
**Léger(ère)** light
**Légumes** vegetables
**Lieu** fish – like cod
**Lièvre** hare
**Limande** lemon sole
**Limon** lime
**Lingue** ling – cod family
**Lit** bed
**Livèche** lovage (like celery)
**Longe** loin
**Lotte (barbot)** burbot – like eel
**Lotte de mer** monkfish, anglerfish
**Lou magret** see *magret*
**Loup de mer** sea-bass
**Lyonnaise (à la)** Lyonnais style: sauce with wine, onions, vinegar
**Macédoine** diced fruit or veg'
**Madeleines** tiny sponge cakes
**Madère** sauce *demi-glace*, Madeira
**Magret (de canard)** breast (of duck)
**Maigre** fish – like sea-bass
**Maillot** carrots, turnips, onions, peas and beans
**Maïs** maize flour
**Maison (de)** of the restaurant
**Maître d'hôtel** sauce with butter, parsley, lemon
**Maltaise (sauce)** orange-flavoured hollandaise sauce
**Manchons** see *goujonnettes*
**Mandarine** tangerine

**Mangetout** peas and pods
**Mangues** mangoes
**Manière (de)** style (of)
**Maquereaux** mackerel
**Maraîchère (à la)** market-gardener style: *velouté* sauce with vegetables
**Marais** marsh or market-garden
**Marbré(e)** marbled
**Marc** pure spirit
**Marcassin** young wild boar
**Marché** market
**Marchand de vin** sauce with red wine, chopped shallots
**Marée** fresh seafood
**Marengo** tomatoes, mushrooms, olive oil, white wine, garlic, herbs
**Marennes (blanches)** oysters, flat shelled
**Marennes (vertes)** green shells
**Mareyeur** fishmonger
**Marinade – mariné(e)** pickled
**Marinière** see *moules*
**Marjolaine** marjoram
**Marjolaine** almond and hazelnut meringue with chocolate cream and praline
**Marmite** stewpot
**Marquise (de)** water ice (of)
**Marrons** chestnuts
**Matelote (d'anguilles)** fresh-water fish stew (or of eels)
**Mauviette** lark
**Médaillon (de)** round piece (of)
**Mélange** mixture or blend
**Melba (à la)** poached peach, with vanilla ice cream, raspberry sauce
**Ménagère (à la)** housewife style: onions, potatoes, peas, turnips, carrots
**Menthe** mint
**Mer** sea
**Merlan** whiting (in Provence – hake)
**Merle** blackbird
**Mérou** grouper (sea fish)
**Merveilles** hot, sugared fritters
**Mesclum** mixture of salad leaves
**Meunière (à la)** sauce with butter, parsley, lemon (sometimes oil)
**Meurette** red wine sauce
**Miel** honey
**Mignardises** *petits fours*
**Mignon (de)** small round piece
**Mignonette** coarsely ground white pepper
**Mijoté(e)** cooked slowly in water
**Milanaise (à la)** Milan style: dipped in breadcrumbs, egg, cheese
**Millassou** sweet maize flour flan
**Mille-feuilles** *1001* thin layers of pastry
**Mimosa** chopped hard-boiled egg
**Mique** stew of dumplings
**Mirabeau** anchovies, olives
**Mirabelles** golden plums
**Mirepoix** cubes of carrots, onion, ham
**Miroton (de)** slices (of)
**Mitonée (de)** soup (of)
**Mode (à la)** in the manner of
**Moelle** beef marrow
**Mojettes** see Poitou-Charentes
**Moka** coffee
**Montagne (de)** from mountains
**Montmorency** with cherries
**Morilles** edible, dark brown, *honeycombed* fungi
**Mornay** cheese sauce
**Morue** cod
**Mostèle (Gâteau de)** cod mousse
**Mouclade** mussel stew
**Moules** mussels
**Moules marinière** mussels cooked in white wine and shallots
**Mousse** cold, light, finely-minced ingredients with cream and egg whites
**Mousseline** hollandaise sauce with whipped cream
**Mousserons** edible fungi
**Moutarde** mustard
**Mouton** mutton
**Mulet** grey mullet
**Mûres** mulberries
**Muscade** nutmeg
**Museau** muzzle
**Myrtilles** bilberries. Blueberries
**Nage (à la)** *court-bouillon*: aromatic poaching liquid
**Nantua** sauce for fish with crayfish, white wine, tomatoes
**Nature** plain
**Navarin** stew, usually lamb
**Navets** turnips
**Nègre** literally *negro*
**Newburg** sauce with lobster, brandy, cream and Madeira
**Nid** nest
**Nivernaise (à la)** Nevers style: carrots and onions
**Noisette** sauce of lightly browned butter
**Noisettes (de)** round pieces (of)
**Noix** nuts
**Noix (de veau)** topside of leg (veal)
**Normande (à la)** Normandy style: fish sauce with mussels, shrimps, mushrooms, eggs and cream

**Nouilles** noodles
**Nouveau (nouvelle)** new or young
**Noyau** sweet liqueur from crushed stones (usually cherries)
**Œufs à la coque** soft-boiled eggs
**Œufs à la neige** see *île flottante*
**Œufs à la poêle** fried eggs
**Œufs brouillés** scrambled eggs
**Œufs durs** hard-boiled eggs
**Œufs moulés** poached eggs
**Oie** goose
**Oignon** onion
**Oison rôti** roast gosling
**Omble chevalier** freshwater char: looks like large salmon trout
**Ombre** grayling
**Ombrine** see *maigre* – fish
**Onglet** flank of beef
**Oreilles (de porc)** ears (pigs')
**Orléannaise (à l')** Orléans style: chicory and potatoes
**Orly** dipped in batter, fried and served with tomato sauce
**Orties** nettles
**Ortolan** wheatear (thrush family)
**Os** bone
**Oseille** sorrel
**Ouillat** see Southwest
**Oursins** sea-urchins
**Pailletté (de)** spangled (with)
**Paillettes** pastry straws
**Pain** bread
**Pain doré** bread soaked in milk and eggs and fried
**Paleron** shoulder
**Palmier (cœurs de)** palm hearts
**Palombe** wood pigeon
**Palomête** see *maigre* – fish
**Palourdes** clams
**Pamplemousse** grapefruit
**Panaché** mixed
**Panade** flour or bread paste
**Panais** parsnip
**Pané(e)** breadcrumbed
**Panier** basket
**Pannequets** like *crêpes*, smaller and thicker
**Paon** peacock
**Papillote (en)** cooked in oiled paper (or foil)
**Paquets (en)** in parcels
**Parfait (de)** *perfect*
**Parisienne (à la)** leeks, potatoes
**Parmentier** potatoes
**Pascade** sweet or savoury pancake
**Pascaline (de)** *quenelle (of)*
**Passe-pierres** seaweed
**Pastèque** watermelon
**Pastis (sauce au)** aniseed based
**Pâté** minced meats (of various types) baked. Usually served cold
**Pâte** pastry, dough or batter
**Pâte à choux** cream puff pastry
**Pâte brisée** short crust pastry
**Pâté en croûte** baked in pastry crust
**Pâtes (fraîches)** fresh pasta
**Pâtés (petits) à la Provençale** anchovy and ham turnovers
**Pâtisserie** pastry
**Pâtisson** custard marrow
**Patte** claw, foot, leg
**Paupiettes** thin slices of meat or fish – used to wrap fillings
**Pavé (de)** thick slice (of)
**Paysan(ne) (à la)** country style
**Peau (de)** skin (of)
**Pêche** peach
**Pêcheur** *fisherman*
**Perche** perch
**Perdreau** partridge
**Périgourdine (à la)** sauce *Périgueux* and goose liver
**Périgueux** sauce with truffles, Madeira
**Persil** parsley
**Persillade** mixture chopped parsley, garlic
**Petite marmite** strong consommé with toast and cheese
**Petits fours** miniature cakes, biscuits, sweets
**Petits gris** small snails
**Petits pois** tiny peas
**Pétoncle** small scallop
**Pets de nonne** small soufflé fritters
**Pieds de porc** pig trotters
**Pigeonneau** young pigeon
**Pignons** pine nuts
**Pilau** rice dish
**Pilou** drumstick
**Piments doux** sweet peppers
**Pintade (pintadeau)** guinea-fowl (young guinea-fowl)
**Piperade** omelette or scrambled eggs with tomatoes, peppers, onions, sometimes ham
**Piquante (sauce)** sharp-tasting sauce with shallots, capers, wine
**Piqué** larded
**Pissenlits** dandelion leaves
**Pistaches** green pistachio nuts
**Pistil de safran** saffron (*pistil* from autumn-flowering crocus)
**Pistou** see Côte d'Azur
**Plateau (de)** plate (of)
**Pleurotes** mushrooms
**Plie franche** plaice

**Plombières** sweet with vanilla ice cream, *kirsch*, candied fruit and *crème chantilly*
**Pluches** sprigs
**Pluvier** plover
**Poché(e)-Pochade** poached
**Pochouse** freshwater fish stew with white wine
**Poêlé** fried
**Poire** pear
**Poireaux** leeks
**Pois** peas
**Poisson** fish
**Poitrine** breast
**Poitrine fumée** smoked bacon
**Poitrine salée** unsmoked bacon
**Poivrade** a peppery sauce with wine vinegar, cooked vegetables
**Poivre noir** black pepper
**Poivre rose** red pepper
**Poivre vert** green peppercorns
**Poivrons** sweet peppers
**Pojarsky** minced meat or fish – cutlet shaped and fried
**Polenta** boiled maize flour
**Polonaise** Polish style: with buttered breadcrumbs, parsley, hard-boiled eggs
**Pommade** thick, smooth paste
**Pommes** apples
**Pommes de terre** potatoes
  **à l'anglaise** boiled
  **allumettes** thin and fried
  **boulangère** sliced with onions
  **château** roast
  **dauphine** croquettes
  **duchesse** mashed with egg yolk
  **en l'air** hollow potato puffs
  **frites** fried chips
  **gratinées** browned with cheese
  **Lyonnaise** sautéed with onions
  **vapeur** boiled
**Pomponnette** savoury pastry
**Porc (carré de)** loin of pork
**Porc (côte de)** pork chop
**Porcelet** suckling pig
**Porto (au)** port
**Portugaise (à la)** Portuguese style: fried onions and tomatoes
**Portugaises** oysters with long, deep shells
**Potage** thick soup
**Pot-au-crème** dessert – usually chocolate or coffee
**Pot-au-feu** clear meat broth served with the meat
**Potée** heavy soup of cabbage, beans, etc.
**Pouchouse** see *pochouse*
**Poularde** large hen
**Poulet** chicken
**Poulet à la broche** spit-roasted chicken
**Poulet Basquaise** chicken with tomatoes and peppers
**Poulet de Bresse** corn-fed, white flesh chicken
**Poulet de grain** grain-fed chicken
**Poulette** young chicken
**Poulpe** octopus
**Pounti** small, egg-based, savoury soufflé with bacon or prunes
**Poussin** small baby chicken
**Poutargue** grey mullet roe
**Praires** small clams
**Pralines** caramelised almonds
**Praslin** caramelised
**Primeurs** young vegetables
**Princesse** *velouté* sauce, asparagus tips and truffles
**Printanièr(e) (à la)** garnish of diced vegetables
**Produits (de)** products (of)
**Profiteroles** choux pastry, custard filled puffs
**Provençale (à la)** Provençal style: with tomatoes, garlic, olive oil, etc.
**Pruneaux** prunes
**Prunes** plums
**Purée** mashed
**Quenelles** light dumplings of fish or poultry
**Quetsches** small, purple plums
**Queue de bœuf** oxtail
**Queues** tails
**Quiche (Lorraine)** open flan of cheese, ham or bacon
**Râble de lièvre (lapin)** saddle of hare (rabbit)
**Raclette** scrapings from specially-made and heated cheese
**Radis** radish
**Ragoût** stew, usually meat, but can describe other ingredients
**Raie (bouclée)** skate (type of)
**Raifort** horseradish
**Raisins** grapes
**Ramequin** see *cocotte (en)*
**Ramier** wood pigeon
**Rapé(e)** grated or shredded
**Rascasse** scorpion fish
**Ratafia** brandy and unfermented Champagne. Almond biscuits
**Ratatouille** aubergines, onions, courgettes, garlic, red peppers and tomatoes in olive oil
**Raves** (root) turnips, radishes, etc.
**Ravigote** sauce with onions, herbs, mushrooms, wine vinegar
**Ravioles** ravioli

**Régence** sauce with wine, truffles, mushrooms
**Reine** chicken and cream
**Reines-Claude** greengages
**Reinette** type of apple
**Réjane** chicken consommé with shredded eggs
**Rémoulade** sauce of mayonnaise, mustard, capers, herbs, anchovy
**Rillettes (d'oie)** potted pork (goose)
**Rillons** small cubes of fat pork
**Ris d'agneau** lamb sweetbreads
**Ris de veau** veal sweetbreads
**Rissettes** small sweetbreads
**Rivière** river
**Riz** rice
**Riz a l'impératrice** cold rice pudding
**Robert** sauce *demi-glace*, white wine, onions, vinegar, mustard
**Rocambole** like a shallot
**Rognonnade** veal and kidneys
**Rognons** kidneys
**Romarin** rosemary
**Rossini** see *tournedos*
**Rôti** roast
**Rouelle (de)** round piece or slice
**Rouget** red mullet
**Rouget barbet** red mullet
**Rouille** orange-coloured sauce with peppers, garlic and saffron
**Roulade (de)** roll (of)
**Roulée(s)** rolled (usually *crêpes*)
**Roux** flour, butter base for sauces
**Royans** fresh sardines
**Rutabaga** swede
**Sabayon** sauce of egg yolks, wine
**Sablés** shortbread
**Safran** saffron (see *pistil de*)
**Sagou** sago
**St-Germain** with peas
**St-Hubert** sauce *poivrade*, bacon and cooked chestnuts
**St-Jacques (coquilles)** scallops
**St-Pierre** John Dory
**Saisons (suivant)** depending on the season of the year
**Salade Niçoise** tomatoes, beans, potatoes, black olives, anchovy, lettuce, olive oil, perhaps tuna
**Salade panachée** mixed salad
**Salade verte** green salad
**Salé** salted
**Salicornes** marsh samphire
**Salmigondis** hotchpotch
**Salmis** red wine sauce
**Salpicon** meat or fish and diced vegetables in sauce
**Salsifis** salsify
**Sanciau** thick sweet or savoury pancake
**Sandre** freshwater fish, like perch
**Sang** blood
**Sanglier** wild boar
**Santé** potatoes and sorrel
**Sarcelle** teal
**Sarriette (poivre d'âne)** savory, bitter herb
**Saucisse** freshly-made sausage
**Saucisson** large, dry sausage
**Saucissons cervelas** saveloys
**Sauge** sage
**Saumon** salmon
**Saumon blanc** hake
**Saumon fumé** smoked salmon
**Sauté** browned in butter, oil or fat
**Sauvage** wild
**Savarin** see *baba au rhum*
**Savoyarde** with Gruyère cheese
**Scarole** *endive*
**Scipion** cuttlefish
**Seiches** squid
**Sel** salt (see *gros sel*)
**Selle** saddle
**Selon grosseur (S.G.)** according to size
**Serpolet** wild thyme
**Sévigné** garnished with mushrooms, roast potatoes, lettuce
**Smitane** sauce with sour cream, onions, white wine
**Soissons** with white beans
**Sole à la Dieppoise** sole fillets, mussels, shrimps, wine, cream
**Sole Cardinale** poached fillets of sole, cream sauce
**Sole Dugléré** sole with tomatoes, onions, shallots, butter
**Sole Marguery** sole with mussels, prawns, white wine
**Sole Walewska** *mornay* sauce, truffles and prawns
**Sorbet** water ice
**Soubise** onion sauce
**Soufflé(e)** beaten egg whites, baked (with sweet or savoury ingredients)
**Soupière** soup tureen
**Soupion** small inkfish
**Sourdons** cockles
**Souvaroff** a game bird with *foie gras* and truffles
**Spaghettis (de)** thin strips (of)
**Spoom** frothy water ice
**Strasbourgeoise (à la)** Strasbourg style: *foie gras*, *choucroute*, bacon
**Sucre** sugar
**Suppions** small cuttlefish
**Suprême** sweet white sauce

**Suprême** boneless breast of poultry – can also describe a fillet of fish
**Talleyrand** truffles, cheese, *foie gras*
**Tanche** tench
**Tapé(e)** dried
**Tartare** raw minced beef
**Tartare (sauce)** sauce with mayonnaise, onions, capers, herbs
**Tarte** open flan
**Tarte Tatin** *upside down* apple tart
**Terrine** baked minced meat or fish, served cold
**Tête de veau vinaigrette** calf's head *vinaigrette*
**Thé** tea
**Thermidor** grilled lobster with browned *béchamel* sauce
**Thon** tunny fish
**Thym** thyme
**Tiède** mild or lukewarm
**Tilleul** lime blossom
**Timbale** mould in which contents are steamed
**Tomates** tomatoes
**Topinambours** Jerusalem artichokes
**Torte** sweet-filled flan
**Tortue** turtle
**Tortue** sauce with various herbs, tomatoes, Madeira
**Toulousaine (à la)** Toulouse style: truffles, *foie gras*, sweetbreads, kidneys
**Tournedos** fillet steak (small end)
**Tournedos chasseur** with shallots, mushrooms, tomatoes
**Tournedos Dauphinoise** with creamed mushrooms, *croûtons*
**Tournedos Rossini** with goose liver, truffles, port, *croûtons*
**Tourte (Tourtière)** covered savoury tart
**Tourteaux** large crabs
**Tranche** slice
**Tranches de bœuf** steaks
**Tripes à la mode de Caen** tripe stew
**Tripettes** small tripe
**Trompettes de la mort** fungi
**Trou** water ice
**Truffée** with truffles
**Truffes** truffles – black, exotic tubers
**Truite** trout
**Truite (au bleu)** trout poached in water and vinegar – turns blue!
**Truite saumonée** salmon trout
**Tuiles** tiles (thin almond slices)
**Turbot (turbotin)** turbot
**Vacherin** ice cream, meringue, cream
**Valenciennes (à la)** rice, red peppers, onions, tomatoes, white wine
**Vallée d'Auge** sauce with Calvados and cream
**Vapeur (à la)** steamed
**Veau** veal
**Veau à la Viennoise (escalope de)** slice of veal with chopped egg
**Veau Milanaise (escalope de)** with macaroni, tomatoes, ham, mushrooms
**Veau pané (escalope de)** thin slice of veal in flour, eggs and breadcrumbs
**Velouté** white sauce with *bouillon* and white *roux*
**Velouté de volaille** thick chicken soup
**Venaison** venison
**Ventre** belly or breast
**Vernis** clams
**Véronique** grapes, wine, cream
**Verte** green mayonnaise with chervil, spinach, tarragon
**Vert-pré** thinly-sliced chips, *maître d'hôtel* butter, watercress
**Verveine** verbena
**Vessie (en)** cooked in a pig's bladder – usually chicken
**Viande** meat
**Vichy** glazed carrots
**Vichyssoise** creamy potato, leek soup – served cold
**Vierge** (sauce) olive oil sauce
**Vierge** literally *virgin*
**Vigneron** wine-grower
**Vinaigre (de)** wine vinegar or vinegar of named fruit
**Vinaigre de Jerez** sherry vinegar
**Vinaigrette (à la)** French dressing with wine vinegar, oil, etc.
**Volaille** poultry
**Vol au vent** puff pastry case
**Xérès (vinaigre de)** sherry (vinegar)
**Yaourt** yoghourt
**Zeste (d'orange)** rubbing from (orange skin)

*If you come across any terms not in the glossary ask for the constituent parts to be written down; translate them using these pages. Example:* **sauce gribiche** *three of the ingredients you'll recognise – mayonnaise, capers and herbs. The other ingredients of* **œufs durs (hachis)** *and* **cornichons** *can be translated easily.*

# *Apéritifs, wines and waters*

*Apéritifs of France*

**Alcohol-based** most common are the *aniseed* ones: **Berger Blanc** and **Pernod** 45 (coloured) – these contain no liquorice. The *pastis apéritifs* do have it: **Berger Pastis, Pernod Pastis 51, Ricard 45.** Drink them with cool water (not ice) – one part to five parts water; initial alcohol content of 45 per cent is then reduced to safe levels.

Other alcohol-based drinks are the *amers, bitters* and *gentians* – 20 per cent. Extracts of various plants are used: **Picon** and **Mandarin** are *amers* – long drinks, one part to two parts water. *Bitters* are extra-bitter: **St-Raphaël Bitter** is one. **Suze** and **Aveze** are *gentian* based.

**Wine-based** *(aromatised wines)* some are *quinquinas* (tropical tree bark); usually red, drunk straight or as a long drink with soda. Main ones are based on Roussillon wines: **Ambassadeur, Byrrh, Dubonnet, St-Raphaël.** Alcohol content 16–18 per cent.

Others are *vermouths*; usually white, dry and *aromatised* by bitter substances – reds are white wine coloured with caramel. Main centres are Chambéry (page 65) and Languedoc: examples **Noilly-Prat, Clarac, Valtoni, Cazapra, Chambérizette** – Chambéry *vermouth* with strawberry juice.

**Natural sweet wines** *(vins doux naturels)* – **Liqueur wines**

See regions: Languedoc-Roussillon, Poitou-Charentes, Provence.

*The types and shades of wines*

**White** wine is made from white or red grapes – the skins are removed at the start of the wine-making process.

**Rosé** is wine from red grapes – juice is separated from skins after a brief period – fermentation is completed without them: *vin gris* (grey) is pale pink – skins and juice kept apart at pressing.

**Red** end product of red grape juice and skins which ferment together.

**Dry** wine is the end product of allowing fermentation to run its whole course – all sugar converts to alcohol.

**Sweet** wine results when fermentation is prematurely stopped – while sugar remains; this done by filtration or adding sulphur dioxide.

**Sparkling** wine results when juice is bottled before fermentation is complete; it finishes in bottle – hence the carbon dioxide bubbles.

*Méthode champenoise* is difficult, lengthy process; fermentation is helped by adding yeast and sugar. Dom Pérignon invented the process. Madame Clicquot developed the technique of keeping it clear and sparkling. To compensate dryness, a *dosage* (sweetening) is added.

**Brandies** Cognac is the end product of distilled white wine; first heated, the vapour is collected and condensed – process is repeated. Armagnac is distilled once. **Fines** – brandies from wine-making areas.

**Marc** is pure spirit, distilled from grape pulp after pressing.

**Eaux-de-vie** read notes in Alsace region (page 19).

*Still and sparkling waters of France*

**Badoit** a sparkling water from St-Galmier, west of Lyon (page 48).

**Evian** a pure, still water. From Evian on Lake Geneva (page 65).

**Perrier** a sparkling water. From a spring at Vergèze, between Lunel and Nîmes (page 62); gases of volcanic origin mix with spring waters. Distinctive, green club-shaped bottle.

**Vichy** another sparkling spring water. From Vichy (page 50).

**Vittel** a still water from the spa, south of Nancy (page 29).

**Volvic** a still water from the Auvergne (page 50).

# *What Wines with What Food*

**Don't** take wines too seriously – enjoy them. **Don't** be dogmatic about combinations – experiment with local wines and surprise yourself. **Don't** drink good, expensive wines with acid foods, highly-spiced foods, with eggs or salads with sharp dressings.

| | Shellfish – Fish Charcuterie | Fish (Sauced) | White Meats Mild Cheeses | Red Meats Strong Cheeses | Game | Desserts |
|---|---|---|---|---|---|---|
| **Alsace** (page 19) | | | | | | |
| Dry whites: **Riesling, Sylvaner, Pinot Blanc, Tokay, Traminer** | • | • | • | | | |
| Medium-sweet whites: **Tokay, Traminer** | | • | | | | • |
| Light red: **Pinot Noir** | • | • | • | • | • | |
| Dessert wine: **Muscat** (*sec*) | | | | | | • |
| **Berry-Bourbonnais** (page 21) | | | | | | |
| Whites: **St-Pourçain, Reuilly, Quincy** | • | • | • | | | |
| Reds: **St-Pourçain, Châteaumeillant** | • | • | • | • | • | |
| **Brittany** (page 23) | | | | | | |
| Dry whites: **Muscadet, Gros Plant du Pays Nantais, Vins de Pays** | • | • | • | | | |
| Reds: **Coteaux d'Ancenis, Vins de Pays** | • | • | • | • | • | |
| **Burgundy** (page 25) | | | | | | |
| Dry whites: **Chablis, Meursault, Viré, Pouilly-Fuissé, St-Véran, Mâcon** and many more; great and humble | • | • | • | | | |
| Rosés: **Marsannay, Irancy** | • | | • | | | |
| Light reds: some **Côte de Beaune** wines, **Mercurey, Givry, Mâcon Supérieur, Gd-Ordinaire, Passetoutgrains,** etc. | • | • | • | • | • | |
| Full-bodied reds: some **Côte de Beaune** and any **Côte de Nuits** wines . . . | | | | • | • | |
| **Champagne-Ardenne** (page 30) | | | | | | |
| Champagne *brut* or *sec* | • | • | • | • | • | • |
| *demi-sec* | | | | | | • |
| Still whites: **Cramant, Chouilly** | • | | • | | | |
| Rosés: **Rosé des Riceys, Côtes de Toul** | • | | • | | | |
| Reds: **Bouzy, Vertus, Damery** | | | • | • | • | |
| **Corsica** (page 73) | | | | | | |
| Dry whites: **Figari** | • | • | • | | | |
| Rosés: **Patrimonio** | • | | • | | | |
| Reds: **Coteaux d'Ajaccio, Sartène** | • | • | • | • | • | |
| Dessert wines: **Muscat, Malvoisie** | | | | | | • |
| **Côte d'Azur** (page 33) | | | | | | |
| Whites: **Côtes de Provence, Cassis** | • | • | • | | | |
| Rosés: **Côtes de Provence, Cassis** | • | | • | | | |
| Reds: **Bandol, Ch. Vignelaure** | | | | • | • | |
| **Dordogne** (page 36) | | | | | | |
| Dry whites: **Bergerac, Côtes de Duras** | • | • | • | | | |
| Sweet whites: **Monbazillac** | | • | | | | • |
| Rosés: **Gaillac** | • | | • | | | |
| Light reds: **Bergerac, Frontonnais, Marmandais, Lavilledieu, Gaillac** | • | • | • | • | • | |
| Full-bodied reds: **Cahors** | | | | • | • | |
| Sparkling: **Gaillac** – *brut* or *sec* | • | | • | | | |
| *demi-sec* | | | | | | • |
| **Hautes-Alpes** (page 37) | | | | | | |
| **Ile de France** (page 38) | | | | | | |
| **Jura** (page 41) | | | | | | |
| Dry whites: **Arbois, Côtes du Jura, Château-Châlon** | • | • | • | | | |

If a dish is prepared with a specific wine (including fish in a red wine sauce) **do** order a similar wine to accompany it. **Do** ask questions and **do** drink local wines with local cheeses. **Do** please treat these two pages as guidelines . . . **Santé!**

| | Shellfish – Fish Charcuterie | Fish (Sauced) | White Meats Mild Cheeses | Red Meats Strong Cheeses | Game | Desserts |
|---|---|---|---|---|---|---|
| **Jura** (continued) | | | | | | |
| Rosés: **Arbois** | ● | | ● | | | |
| Sparkling: **L'Etoile, Arbois** | ● | | ● | | | |
| **Languedoc-Roussillon** (page 43) | | | | | | |
| Dry whites: **Clairette du Languedoc and Bellegarde, Vins de Pays** | ● | ● | ● | | | |
| Light/medium reds: **Costières du Gard, Coteaux du Languedoc** (all villages), **Minervois, Corbières, Vins de Pays** | ● | ● | ● | ● | ● | |
| Full-bodied reds: **Fitou, Roussillon** | | | | ● | ● | |
| Sparkling: **Blanquette de Limoux** | ● | | ● | | | |
| Dessert wines: **Banyuls, Maury, Rivesaltes, Frontignan** | | | | | | ● |
| **Loire** (page 45) | | | | | | |
| Dry whites: **Sancerre, Fumé, Reuilly, Quincy, Vouvray, Savennières** | ● | ● | ● | | | |
| Sweet whites: **Vouvray, Bonnezeaux** | | ● | | | | ● |
| Rosés *sec:* **Touraine, Rosé de Loire** | ● | | ● | | | |
| *demi-sec:* **Rosé/Cabernet d'Anjou** | ● | | | | | ● |
| Reds: **Chinon, Bourgueil, Gamay** | ● | ● | ● | ● | ● | |
| Sparkling *brut* or *sec* | ● | | ● | | | |
| *demi-sec* | | | | | | ● |
| **Lyonnais** (page 48) | | | | | | |
| Whites: **Vins du Bugey** | ● | ● | ● | | | |
| Reds: **Beaujolais, Côte Roannaise** | ● | ● | ● | ● | ● | |
| **Massif Central** (page 52) | | | | | | |
| Reds: **Côtes d'Auvergne, Côtes du Forez, Vin de Pays de l'Ardèche** | ● | ● | ● | ● | ● | |
| See Provence for **Côtes du Rhône** wines | | | | | | |
| **Normandy** (page 55) see region | | | | | | |
| **North** (page 57) see region | | | | | | |
| **Poitou-Charentes** (page 60) | | | | | | |
| Dry whites: **Ile de Ré, Haut-Poitou** | ● | ● | ● | | | |
| Reds: **Vins du Haut-Poitou** | ● | ● | ● | ● | ● | |
| Dessert wine: **Pineau des Charentes** | | | | | | ● |
| **Provence** (page 62) | | | | | | |
| Whites: **Cassis, Côtes de Provence** | ● | ● | ● | | | |
| Rosés: **Lirac, Tavel** | ● | | ● | | | |
| Full-bodied reds: **Côtes du Rhône, Côte Rôtie, Hermitage, Cornas** | | | | ● | ● | |
| Sparkling *brut:* **Die, St-Péray** | ● | | ● | | | |
| *demi-sec:* **Die** | | | | | | ● |
| Dessert wines: **Beaumes de Venise** | | | | | | ● |
| **Savoie** (page 65) | | | | | | |
| Dry whites: **Seyssel, Crépy** | ● | ● | ● | | | |
| Rosés: **Savoie** | ● | | ● | | | |
| Reds: **Mondeuse, Chautagne, Gamay** | ● | ● | ● | ● | ● | |
| Sparkling: **Seyssel** | ● | | ● | | | |
| **Southwest** (page 68) | | | | | | |
| Dry whites: **Graves, Tursan, E-D-Mers** | ● | ● | ● | | | |
| Sweet whites: **Sauternes, Jurançon** | | ● | | | | ● |
| Medium reds: **Graves, Médoc,** others | ● | ● | ● | ● | ● | |
| Full-bodied reds: **St-Emilion, Madiran** | | | | ● | ● | |

# *Index of Wines*

# *Index of Cheeses*

*This Index does not pretend to be a definitive list of French cheeses; many others are very rarely seen and some are very closely related to the list above. Do take all the advice given on page 10 — try as many of the different varieties as you can. Make waiters identify all the cheeses offered at restaurants – and ask for* **une bouchée** *(a mouthful) of as many types as possible; don't be prejudiced about any of them – many taste better than they look.*

## So you think you know that road sign?

*(Compiled by Shirley Clancy)*

**Absence d'accotements** no verges
**Absence de glissières latérales** no protective barriers
**Absence de marquage** no road markings
**Absence de signalement horizontal** no road markings
**Absence de signalement vertical** no road signs
**Accotement étroit** narrow verge
**Accotement non stabilisé/impraticable** soft verges
**Affaissement** subsidence
**Aire** rest area/lay-by
**Allumez vos feux** switch on lights
**Arbres inclinés** trees leaning over the road
**Arrosage et boue** watering – mud on the road
**Atelier d'entretien** maintenance workshop
**Attachez vos ceintures** fasten your seat belts
**Attente de marquage** no road markings
**Attention (!)** look out (!)
**Attention aux travaux** danger – road works
**Autoroute péage** toll motorway
**Autres directions** other directions
**Bande d'arrêt d'urgence** emergency hard shoulder
**Bande d'arrêt d'urgence déformée** emergency hard shoulder – bad surface
**Betteraves** beet harvesting – mud on road
**Bifurcation** road divides
**Bouchon** bottleneck – traffic jam
**Boue** mud
**Brouillard** fog or mist
**Carrefour** crossroads
**Cédez le passage** give way
**Centre d'entretien** maintenance centre
**Centre ville** town centre
**Chantier** roadworks
**Chantier mobile** 'mobile' roadworks
**Chaussée deformée** bad road surface
**Chaussée inondable** road liable to flooding
**Chute de pierres** danger – falling rocks or stones
**Circulation alternée** single line traffic – alternately
**Convoi exceptionnel** large load
**Dans l'agglomération** built-up area
**Déviation** diversion
**Eboulements** landslides
**En cas de pluie** when raining
**Enquête de circulation** traffic census
**Essence** petrol – gasoline (2 star)
**Eteignez voz phares** switch off headlights
**Fauchage** mowing
**Feux** traffic lights
**Feux clignotants** flashing lights
**Fin de . . . .** end of . . . .
**Flèches vertes** green arrows (secondary route)
**Gendarmerie** traffic and local police
**Gravillons** loose chippings
**Hauteur limitée** height limited
**Hors des cases** (accompanied by sign) no parking outside bays
**Interdiction de stationner** parking prohibited
**Interdit** prohibited
  **aux piétons** no entry to pedestrians
  **du 1er au 15 du mois** no parking from 1st to 15th of month
  **du 16 à fin de mois** no parking from 16th to end of month
  **sauf aux livraisons** no entry except for deliveries
  **sauf aux riverains** no entry except for residents
  **sauf services** no entry except for service vehicles
  **sur accotement** no stopping on verges
**Itinéraire bis** secondary route
**Itinéraire conseillé** recommended route
**Itinéraire obligatoire** compulsory route
**Laissez libre la bande d'arrêt d'urgence** do not obstruct hard shoulder
**Libre service** self-service
**Mairie** town hall
**Mouvements de chars** heavy vehicles
**Nappe d'eau** puddles on road
**Nappe de fumée** smoke patches
**Ni vitesse ni bruit** drive slowly and quietly
**Nids de poules** pot holes
**P** parking
**P.T.T. (P et T)** post office and telephone
**Par temps de pluie** during rain
**Passage à niveau** level crossing

**Passage protégé** you have right of way
**Péage** toll
**Piétons** pedestrians
**Pique-nique** picnic area
**Pique-nique jeux d'enfants** picnic area with playground
**Piste cyclable** cycle lane
**Poids lourds** heavy/long vehicles
**Priorité à droite** give way to traffic coming from your right
**Prochaine sortie** next exit
**Prudence** take care
**Rainurage** grooves in road
**Ralentissez** slow down
**Rappel** reminder (accompanied by instruction: e.g. speed limit)
**Renseignements** information
**Respectez les feux** obey traffic lights
**Risque de brouillard** possible fog
**Risque d'inondation** flooding risk
**Risque de verglas** possible risk of ice (usually 'black ice') on road
**Route barrée** road closed
**Route bombée** badly cambered road (usually bumps in road)
**Route glissante** slippery road
**Sens interdit** no entry
**Sens unique** one-way street
**Serrez à droite/gauche** keep to the right/left
**Servez-vous** help yourself (petrol – gasoline)
**Signal automatique** automatic signal
**Sortie** exit
  **de camions** lorries emerging
  **de carrière** quarry exit
  **d'Ecole** children emerging
  **d'engins** machinery or plant emerging
  **de secours** emergency exit
  **d'usine** factory exit
  **de véhicules** traffic exit
**Stationnement alterné semi-mensuel** parking alternates half-monthly
**Stationnement génant** park 'tidily' – do not obstruct
**Stationnement interdit** no parking
**Super** petrol – gasoline (4 star)
**Toutes directions** all directions
**Travaux** roadworks
**Travaux cachent les hommes** roadworks obscuring men
**Traversée de véhicules** vehicles crossing the road
**Trou (en formation)** hole in the road (developing)
**Troupeaux** cattle
**Un train peut en cacher au autre** (seen at level crossings) one train may be concealing another coming in the opposite direction
**Véhicules lents** slow vehicles
**Véhicules lents serrez à droite** slow vehicles keep to the right
**Véhicules lents voie de droite** slow vehicles use right hand lane
**Vendange** grape harvesting
**Vent latéral** cross wind
**Vent violent** strong cross winds
**Verglas fréquent** often icy
**Virages** bends
**Virages en épingle à cheveux** hairpin bends
**Virages en d'envers** bends with opposite or reverse camber
**Virages sur (km)** bends for (km)
**Voie sans issue** no through road
**Zône bleue** parking for permit (disc) holders only in a 'blue zone' (you need a 'disc' obtained locally from newsagents)

**Do**

drive on the right
wear seat belts and put under-tens in the back seat
take a red warning triangle for emergency breakdowns
adjust your headlights for right-hand driving
take a complete set of spare bulbs for your car
give priority to vehicles coming from the right – especially at roundabouts – unless road markings or signs indicate otherwise
observe speed limits:
  built-up areas 60 kmh – 37 mph
  ordinary roads 90 kmh – 56 mph (if **wet** 80 kmh – 50 mph)
  dual carriageways and toll-free motorways 110 kmh – 68 mph (if **wet** 80 kmh – 50 mph)
  all motorways 130 kmh – 81 mph (if **wet** 110 kmh – 68 mph)

**Do not**

stop on *any* road unless you can pull right off the carriageway
drive with a provisional licence – or if under 18 years old